SHOULD WE

MARRY?

SHOULD WE

MARRY?

Joseph M. Champlin

ave maria press   Notre Dame, Indiana

Nihil Obstat:
Most Rev. Thomas J. Costello, DD
Censor Deputatus

Imprimatur:
Most Rev. James M. Moynihan, DD
Bishop of Syracuse, New York
Given at Syracuse, NY on 1 January 2001.

The *Nihil Obstat* and *Imprimatur* are official declarations that a book or pamphlet is free of doctrinal error. No implication is contained therein that those who have granted the *Nihil Obstat* and *Imprimatur* agree with the contents, opinions, or statements expressed.

---

www.avemariapress.com

International Standard Book Number: 0-87793-711-7

Cover and text design by Brian C. Conley

Printed and bound in the United States of America.

Library of Congress Cataloging-in-Publication Data
    Champlin, Joseph M.
    Should we marry? / Joseph M. Champlin.
       p. cm.
    Includes bibliographical references.
    ISBN 0-87793-711-7 (pbk.)
    1. Marriage--Religious aspects--Catholic Church. I. Title.
    BX2250 .C488 2001
    248.4--dc21

                                      2001001197
                                          CIP

CONTENTS

INTRODUCTION

Patricia and Michael met and became a couple at a New England college. After graduation, he went to law school in New York City and she returned home to pursue a master's degree at the local university.

The courtship continued at a distance over those graduate-student years. Later, Michael passed the bar exam and accepted a position at the district attorney's office in Patricia's home city. Patricia, in the meantime, had shifted her career orientation, became a nurse, and began working at an area hospital in the pediatric oncology unit. Both jobs, his and hers, were time-consuming and energy-draining. Then, soon after their engagement, Patricia's father died suddenly and unexpectedly of a massive heart attack.

Prior to the wedding, both composed their hopes and expectations for the marriage, letters to be used as part of the homily at the nuptial service. Patricia's went like this:

> *My Dearest Mike:*
>
> *I knew the first time I met you that you were a special person. In the ten years I've known you, I've seen you do some extraordinary things. It's not what you've done over the years that makes me love you as much as*

I do today. It's the person you are that makes me love you as much as I do today—and know I will for the rest of our lives together. It's the values you hold dear and the love you give me from your heart. You are my best friend. You bring joy and beauty to my life. You make me feel good about myself. You make our time spent together special, wonderful, and memorable. You make me look forward to our future together. You listen to me when I'm hurting. You hug me when you know I need it most. You forgive me when I am wrong. You laugh with me. You cried with me when my dad died and held my hand. You dream with me about what our future will hold. You hope with me that things will go well. And when they don't, because they can't always, you sit with me, you pray with me, you stand by me. We get through things together. We will always get through and go through life together, side by side.

I love you,
Patricia

Michael's hopes and expectations were shorter, but similar and to the point.

Dear Patricia:

As I think about my hopes and expectations, I am thinking back over the last ten years to the day we first met. We have come such a long way since our days in college. Each year has been better than the last. And each year I know we have grown closer, and our relationship has grown stronger.

You have become my best friend in the world. My hope and expectation is that we continue to grow closer and always be best friends. I know you will be a great mother, and I look forward to starting a family

8

together. But most of all I look forward to marrying
you, and spending our lives together.
I know I don't say it nearly enough:

I love you Patricia,
Michael

* * *

Over the past decade I have stood at an altar and listened to more than five hundred couples proclaim their
nuptial vows.

The spoken words of every promise were almost exactly identical: "For better, for worse, for richer, for poorer, in
sickness and in health, in good times and in bad, I will love
you and honor you all the days of my life until death do us
part."

Each of those church services likewise had very similar
basic patterns or structures to them.

Yet, at least in the Roman Catholic church over the past
quarter of a century, there has been a uniqueness about all
of those marriage ceremonies. Couples have stamped their
individual personalities upon the details.

By selecting readings, prayers, and blessings from a rich
resource of alternatives; by asking people close to them—
family and friends—to take an active part in the celebration
itself as readers, ushers, servers, and the like; by arranging
special music expressive of their love and dreams; even by
writing brief descriptions of their own hopes and expectations for their wedded future, like those of Mike and
Patricia; by incorporating all or some of these elements in
the preparation process, the bride and groom have made
their nuptial celebration in church like everyone else's wedding, but still different from all others. They have made it
distinctly their own, a reflection of them.

This singular nature or specialness of the developed
nuptial rite appropriately fits today's marriages. Those
many weddings at which I have participated represent the

coupling of one thousand individuals. All of those brides and grooms are unique persons. Each one possesses identifying fingerprints. Each one was assigned, probably soon after birth, a specifying Social Security number. Each one received at conception a God-created particular soul, unlike the soul of any other person, which gave the person life, and an inner energy or fire, as well as a power to channel everyday activities in a positive direction.

Moreover, when such unique persons forge a relationship and eventually emerge as a married pair, they necessarily constitute a singular couple. There is no other like them. That specialness continues when husband and wife become father and mother. The child or children borne of their love are likewise unique. Only the two of them together could produce this particular child or these particular children.

This uniqueness of the two individuals and of the resulting relationship means that encounters with them are both rich and complex. Nevertheless, these pairs of people, special as they are, need in our day to deal with three common major issues.

IS THIS THE PERSON FOR ME?

Courtships now tend to be much longer than they were during my first period in the priesthood forty-five years ago. Often the pattern moves in this fashion: Acquaintances become friends become lovers and then ponder marriage. As the relationship deepens, each one within often asks: Is this really the one for me? Do I want to spend the rest of my life with him? Will I be content growing old with her? Would she be a great mother, he a great father of my, of our, children?

SHOULD WE LIVE TOGETHER FIRST?

A second issue faced by couples today is whether to live together before marriage. For various reasons—for example, convenience, economics, cultural pressure, desire for intimacy, testing of the relationship—the number of engaged couples living together before marriage has geometrically increased during the past two decades.

The decision to do so usually involves some self-doubts or anxiety upon their part and in some instances opposition or lack of acceptance from others, especially parents.

WILL YOU MARRY ME?

The third issue is not a new one but one that couples have always faced: how to ask the big question. Despite a recent shift away from traditional values and customs, most of the engaged couples in my last ten years of experience have opted for these older standard engagement procedures: seeking permission from the father (or mother, or both); selecting a memorable place or occasion; proposing on bended knee.

During the initial interview with those more than five hundred couples, I began with some ice-breaking questions: Where do you work? How did you meet? Who was the first one to say "I love you"? What was the engagement proposal like?

The conversation usually flows freely and the details are for me both interesting and informative. They are also helpful later in preparing for the wedding ceremony itself.

The various creative ways in which prospective grooms proposed to their beloved struck me several years ago as remarkably touching, sometimes humorous, and often inspirational. I began to make notes afterward about each proposal and found that others, particularly the engaged, were intrigued by these accounts.

This book grew out of those encounters and subsequent notes. I contacted people like Michael and Patricia—some now married, some awaiting their wedding day—and asked permission to use their own stories. Names generally have been changed and some details adjusted to provide a certain degree of privacy for those couples. Moreover, they all had opportunities to read the text involving them before it became part of this book.

I pray that their stories and my observations will assist others in love who are wrestling with those three major issues. Some questions at the end of each section may help you focus your own thoughts and arrive at wise answers to these three concerns.

PART ONE

IS THIS THE PERSON FOR ME?

CHAPTER 1

FRIENDSHIP

Tim, in his middle thirties, has worked as a funeral director since graduation from school and the subsequent apprenticeship. Personable, sensitive, and proficient, he is well liked by the local clergy and highly respected by his professional colleagues.

After the typical career start-up as a full-time employee at an established home and part-time work assisting other directors, Tim launched his own funeral business in a small village. Building up the necessary clientele to provide sufficient "calls" for a financially stable venture of this type is a slow process. He thus needed and still needs to augment his income by a substantial amount of freelance service for other funeral directors.

His funeral home sponsors an area softball team, and one night he joined the players with their friends for a post-game celebration at a popular local emporium. That evening event changed the direction of Tim's life.

He met Clare there, ten years younger and a graduate student at the local university hoping to become an elementary school teacher. Smitten, but shy and cautious, Tim asked if she might like to earn some spending money by occasionally cleaning his funeral home.

Clare agreed, and at the end of her first Saturday working for him, Tim nervously made an offer: "Would you like to go out for something to eat?" The student, would-be teacher, cleaning woman responded positively, and their meal together seemed to go well. However, Clare failed to telephone him during the next week. Tim, having known some rejections in the past, felt downcast, assuming she had no interest in developing more than a working relationship.

But eventually Clare surprised him with a follow-up call, suggesting that they do a repeat of the work/dinner scenario because she enjoyed the last experience very much.

Tim's spirits naturally soared. Those combination connections then became a regular occurrence and the relationship grew. Three years later Tim and Clare were at their parish church arranging a wedding date.

After about twenty minutes of informal and light conversation with the clergyman about their work and their initial encounter, about the courtship and the forthcoming marriage, the priest posed this question to Clare: "So you want to marry Tim—why him?"

She blushed a little, but then replied: "We are best friends. I can tell him anything. He is always there for me now, and I know he will be there for me in the future. But above all Tim is a very caring, unselfish person, always thinking of others and concerned about them, both in his professional work and in his personal life."

Tim could sense that the spotlight would soon switch to him, and thus he was not surprised when the priest gently inquired: "Why Clare?"

"For all the reasons she just gave. However, Clare is also very patient and understanding. She doesn't complain when my work interferes with what we had planned to do."

"For example," Tim continued, "we recently drove several hundred miles to visit my sister in New England. We were there only six hours when the phone rang telling me about a death and consequent 'call' back home. We had to pack up immediately and return. There were no complaints, no grumbling on her part."

He went on, "Even my plan for giving her the engagement ring on Christmas Eve went awry because of the business. I had the diamond wrapped in a special way and placed on the tree as part of the decorations. I also had in mind exactly how I was going to propose.

"However, the phone rang and I learned that a young man, a close friend, had died. That meant, I knew, that all of Christmas Eve would be spent with his family. This messed up all my carefully made plans. But, once again, Clare never grumbled or complained."

Those who marry persons like physicians or funeral directors need to recognize that in married life they and the children quite probably will be sharing the time, energy, and heart of their spouses and parents with others. Critically ill patients or survivors of unexpected deaths will understandably demand their part of them.

Clare, at this point, seemed to grasp that truth. In fact, Tim's response on those two occasions merely underscored or illustrated for her the kind of concerned and caring person he is, the qualities that make him lovable and the man she wishes to marry.

When asked why they wish to marry each other, engaged couples in the past decade have almost universally responded with one word: friendship. "He is my best friend." "She is my soul mate, my closest friend." That certainly was the case with Clare and Tim.

What does it mean to be or have a friend? I hear repeatedly from the engaged these symptoms, experiences, or descriptions of friendship:

"I can tell him anything." "She is the first one I call when I am up or down, when something good has just happened or something bad troubles me." "She is always there for me." "He respects me and treats me like a queen." "We get along great." "We like many of the same things." "We enjoy being together."

The dictionary definition of a friend translates those concrete descriptions into abstract terms: "One that seeks the society or welfare of another whom he (she) holds in affection, respect, or esteem or whose companionship and personality are pleasurable: an intimate associate, especially when other than a lover or relative."[1]

Friends are not necessarily lovers. Today, however, as I have mentioned, almost all the engaged cite friendship as the key ingredient of their relationship. Still, they would also consider several other persons as friends although not in the same category or to the same degree as their intended spouses.

Friendship has an illusive and mystical quality. It just happens. A comfortable connection simply develops. We enjoy another's presence. We like this man or woman.

We often use the term rather loosely. "All our friends are here." But a true friend is a precious gift, and each individual in a lifetime probably has at most five or six such treasured friends. Yet we have many persons with whom we are friendly. In addition, the level of friendship varies with each relationship.

A generic love spawns friendships, sustains them, deepens them, and, in the case of engaged couples, takes them to different levels with unique characteristics. We need, therefore, now to explore the nature of love.

THE NATURE OF LOVE

Love, as the old popular song noted, is a "many splendored thing."

During a given day we might make all of these statements: "I love pizza and a beer." "I love rainbows." "I love my horse." "I love my job." "I love working with people in need, like little kids." "I love dad, mom, and my grandparents." "I love you."

The word clearly has many meanings.

Sometimes we link love with positive feelings and warm emotions. "You make me feel so good." However, love based solely on a fondness for someone or something has a certain self-centered or selfish nature to it. Moreover, love identified with and limited to comforting, fuzzy feelings eliminates both its stability as well as its persistence in tough times.

A close, committed, long-term relationship, a satisfying friendship, or a successful marriage requires an inner attitude that is self-giving or unselfish, as well as steady and sometimes even courageous.

A half-century ago, then world-famous psychoanalyst Erich Fromm wrote that true love is fundamentally and primarily giving. "In the very act of giving, we experience our strength, wealth and power; we experience ourselves as overflowing, spending, alive, and hence joyous."[2]

That notion of love as giving may seem simple, but in fact it is dynamic, personal, and challenging. Every morning we rise aware of some but not all the ways in which situations will demand our giving. Each individual will encounter circumstances uniquely her or his own that call for giving. All of those dynamic situations and personal circumstances will challenge us to self-sacrifice, to unselfishness, to think of another or others instead of ourselves, to consider their needs and wants instead of our own.

For serious followers of Christ, that concept of love as giving sounds very familiar. Jesus taught: "No one has greater love than this, to lay down one's life for one's friends" (Jn 15:13). He went about doing good for others and giving his life on the cross for all. St. Paul, in his classic passage to the Corinthians, which has been the most popular choice for Catholic nuptial services, describes the characteristics of that giving kind of love: "Love is patient, love is kind . . ." (1 Cor 13:4).

The two illustrations which follow may clarify this concept of true love. Both involve the gift of eyesight.

GIVING

Television anchorman Tom Brokaw gained acclaim as a writer when he published *The Greatest Generation*, a book which almost immediately soared to the top of bestseller lists and remained there.

He collected stories of people who "came of age during the Great Depression and the Second World War and went on to build modern America—men and women whose everyday lives of duty, honor, achievement, and courage gave us the world we have today."[3]

One of those stories is about Thomas Broderick, a nineteen-year-old pre-med student in 1942 during the early days of World War II. He undoubtedly could have sought and received a deferment because of his medical studies. Instead, he enlisted first in the merchant marine and then in the army to become an airborne infantryman.

In many situations Tom had the option of safer, self-preserving alternatives, but in each case he chose instead more dangerous, unselfish paths.

After paratrooping into Holland, he was almost immediately thrown into the midst of a battle in which the Germans outnumbered the Allied forces two to one. On the fifth day of the struggle, Tom raised himself above the foxhole to take better aim at an enemy soldier. A bullet pierced his left temple and went cleanly through his head.

A chaplain rushed to him and administered the church's rites for the seriously wounded. Tom was then swiftly transferred to a hospital in England. He survived, a remarkable feat in itself. But when Tom regained consciousness, he couldn't see. A doctor reassured him that when the hemorrhage cleared up, he would be all right.

The army moved him to a hospital in Menlo Park, California, one of two facilities in the nation treating blind veterans. There a doctor bluntly revealed the truth to Tom: he would be blind forever.

At first he wept and wept, then grew angry, disoriented, and bitter. He resisted rehabilitation. Only after frustrating failures in work situations did he accept the necessity of specialized training.

He learned Braille and the insurance business. He also discovered that somehow the blindness had sharpened his sense of hearing and likewise gave him an uncanny ability to identify people who had previously spoken with him. His training, his resurrected enthusiasm, and his natural talents coupled with the rapidly growing nature of the insurance industry led to significant economic successes.

A few years later Tom and his mother traveled to the famous shrine at Lourdes in France seeking a miraculous cure. He prayed for restored eyesight, but also asked the Lord to send him a woman he might marry.

Soon thereafter, at twenty-seven, his second petition was answered. Tom met Eileen, a twenty-three-year-old nurse. She fell in love with him instantly and describes how that giving spirit manifested itself in their early courtship.

> You didn't think about his blindness. It just didn't seem to matter. He ran a business by himself and didn't need help from anyone, although it was a little tricky when we went out alone. I'd have to take him to the men's room and ask someone to take him in. I'd stand outside. I think, being a nurse, I was a little more flexible.

Tom's business continued to flourish. They married, had seven children, owned a large house with many bedrooms, and led lives filled with loving service for others. That included, of course, their own children, but also many different people in need, especially veterans.

Tom shrugs off his efforts for other persons trying to cope with blindness:

> I'd tell them about my own struggle—how I was young when I became blind and I knew how they felt. I brought some of them down to my office so they could see the Braille machine and what was

principal film critic as well. Twenty-five years later he retired from the paper, having gained respect and recognition for his writing and lecturing as well as television work.

Retirement meant some freelance writing, teaching film classes, and occasionally lecturing around the nation. It also brought some decline in his health.

That metal piece lodged in his hip eventually necessitated surgery and a new knee for my brother. A slight stroke brought some minor impairment of speech. Marvelous laser surgery corrected a cataract condition and improved vision in his good eye (the other had been virtually useless for some years).

Soon, however, his eyesight began to decline again. After a thorough examination, his ophthalmologist jolted Chuck with this definitive statement: "Friend, you are now legally blind." Macular degeneration had taken its toll.

At first, he tried to drive, but soon Chuck abandoned that effort. It was too unsettling for him with impaired vision to dodge cars on the busy Los Angeles streets and freeways.

He no longer could see well enough to part his hair, cut his nails, or read a restaurant menu.

For thirty years Chuck would rise early, pick up the *Los Angeles Times* and *New York Times* from the driveway, and speed read through both papers. Not any more. A complex machine enlarges the print, and he can make out the headlines; but his wife of fifty-plus years often reads the details for him.

However, he can still write. In high school my brother learned to touch type, a skill for which now he is extremely grateful. With that ability Chuck can compose on the computer, although Peg needs to read the created text back to him for his approval and corrections.

Chuck naturally continues to struggle with the frustration, anger, and understandable depression that comes with this legally blind condition. Moreover, he must adjust to the rather constant necessity of letting his wife assist him with many tasks. Love as a complex giving-receiving situation is very real to him. He grasps that well and finds himself filled with gratitude for the vision he does have and with compassion for those who are totally without sight.

CHARACTERISTICS OF LOVE

As you contemplate the question "Is this the person for me?" reflect on your relationship and the dynamics of giving and receiving you experience in it. Does it enable you to give of yourself freely like Thomas Broderick? Is it teaching you how to receive love too, as my brother Chuck continues to learn to do?

While the notion of love as giving and receiving contains dynamic, personal, and challenging ingredients, it may be helpful to add several further characteristics of true love to reflect upon as you discern "Is this the person for me?"

Love empowers. A loving person, recognizing another's gifts and talents, seeks with great care and concern to unleash that potential and to bring those attributes to full development.

This, of course, is a primary duty as well as a privilege for each person in a marriage. Doing this for one another will eventually help you do this for your children.

Love responds. This responsiveness means we weep when our beloved weeps and rejoice when he or she rejoices. That entails being an interested listener and sometimes silent companion. In the example in the Introduction, Michael listens when Patricia is hurting, hugs her when she needs it most, laughs with her, cries with her. He held her hand when her dad died.

Love respects. To respect, in this context, means to take one another as you are, not as your partner should be or as you may want the other to be. In some ways this respectful type of love is the most essential ingredient for any successful relationship. That includes marriage, family or work relationships, and, of course, friendships.

Many years ago I had a sharp clash with a colleague just prior to a plane trip for a speaking engagement in a distant city. For several hours during the long journey I was grumbling to myself about the incident. After checking in at the hotel, I went to the speakers' lounge. A friend who happened to be there listened sensitively as I recounted in detail the story of my encounter and the consequent agitated feelings.

Her simple but wise response was: "We can only be upset by others to the degree we let them upset us." A respecting love does not approve of another's troubling and objectively wrong actions but can still accept the other as he or she is, not as we want that person to be or as that person should be. With that approach, we are less liable to allow the actions of others to disturb our inner peace.

Love understands. A loving person goes beneath the surface and asks why when confronted with another's behavior that irritates or confuses. What might be behind this annoying or puzzling action?

While teaching religion some time back to a class of junior high students, I had displayed on the front wall a dozen image-words like rock, water, and wind. The students were to select which one best expressed and which one least expressed who God was to them.

The activity quickly engaged the interest and response of all the boys and girls, except one. Margaret was, instead, toying with her pencil and, head down, paying no attention to the exercise. Slightly annoyed and somewhat puzzled by the lack of response from this bright and otherwise cooperative student, I rather abruptly asked her choice.

She replied: "I forgot my glasses this morning and can't see the words." She was not impudent or recalcitrant, but more likely feeling awkward and uncomfortable.

DISCERNING THE REAL THING

Rosalie Brennan has worked as a public school counselor for about two decades. She and her husband have raised two daughters, both of whom are college graduates, one recently married and the other currently in a serious relationship.

Rosalie has developed a series of questions helping couples (and thus individuals) to discern if they are, as she terms it, "in love or in lust." Is their relationship based on a mature and self-giving love which bodes well for a lifelong successful and satisfying marriage? Or is their relationship based more on a physical and emotional attraction? Such an attraction, however strong, is necessarily ephemeral as well as somewhat self-centered, and does not promise a successful and satisfying marriage.

Here and in the next two chapters I will list some of Rosalie's questions for an individual or the couple to ponder.

1. Is this other person your best friend?
2. Do you attempt to meet the other's needs before you take care of yourself?
3. Do you have similar or complementary values on issues such as family, fidelity, money, lifestyle, children, ambitions, and work ethic?
4. If you were deserted on an island, would this person be the one you would want to be with?
5. Are you intimidated by the other person?
6. Do you feel safe when you are together?
7. Do you walk together, not in front or behind each other?
8. Do you have similar or opposing views about your extended families?
9. Do you both realize that the wedding and marriage is only the beginning of the task of making a happy relationship?
10. What does the other person do to make you happy?

FRIENDSHIP TAKES WORK

Henri J. M. Nouwen wrote more than forty books and is considered one of the great spiritual writers in modern times. He lectured here and abroad, taught at Harvard, Yale, and Notre Dame, and spent the last seven years of his life serving people who have mental handicaps at the l'Arche Community in Toronto.

Sabbatical Journey contains edited excerpts from "The Diary of His Final Year." Prayer and friendship are recurrent themes in that book. Nouwen, for whom friendships were critically important, acknowledges that they involve "hard work" and entail a "real discipline."

In a friendship, he observes, "nothing can be taken for granted, nothing happens automatically, nothing comes without concentrated effort. Friendship requires trust, patience, attentiveness, courage, repentance, forgiveness, celebration, and most of all faithfulness."[6]

A friendship which has grown into a deeper and different love is an ideal start toward a stable and strong marital relationship. Good communication with one another, on the other hand, is an absolutely essential element for a successful marriage. We will now examine this matter of communication.

CHAPTER 2

COMMUNICATION

Ken and Judith courted for two and a half years before their November afternoon wedding. The groom spent more than fifteen years as an officer in the reserves, earned an M.B.A. from a local university, and now has become an acknowledged computer software specialist.

He composed his hopes and expectations for their marriage to be used during the church ceremony.

Dear Judith,

As I stand here today, I can't help but feel truly blessed; blessed to have all our family among us, blessed to have all our friends among us, but most of all blessed to be standing here professing my love to you. I cannot believe that this day has finally come upon us. I have been waiting for this day for thirty-five years and five months. Some may feel we have waited too long, but finding your soul mate is definitely worth the wait. You are my soul mate.

In the past two years, six months, and fourteen days we have grown so much together. You have taught me so much and have made me who I am today. You have taught me to love, to listen, to understand, and to communicate. I know that in the past, my life was work, work, work, but you have given me so many reasons to enjoy my life and enjoy my life with you. I never knew how much I could love someone and have someone love me as much as you do.

When I am not with you or I'm away from you, I cannot wait to reach out and touch your face and hold on to you for dear life. I can't wait to hear your voice call out that silly little nickname you've given me, which we will not mention here. You are the epitome of everything I have dreamed that a woman, friend, companion, lover, and wife would be. Somebody upstairs really likes me. You make me feel so special and worthwhile, you are truly a part of me that makes me whole.

From the first moment I met you, I knew that we would be together for the rest of our lives. I think of all the special times we have spent together since that wonderful day in April. I know that we have had some differences, but we have always proved that we could overcome them. We have had some wonderful times together, and I so look forward to having more wonderful times.

We owe so much to our family and friends for their wonderful friendship and guidance, and because of them we understand the true meaning of family and friendship.

I love you, Judith, with all my heart and soul.

Your loving husband and best friend,
Kenneth

After graduating from college and working a few secretarial jobs, Judith joined her mother's insurance and investment firm. Serious about jogging, Judith ran a marathon in

Bermuda to raise funds for someone with leukemia. Her hopes and expectations stress, among other elements, the critical importance of good communication for a successful marriage.

My Dearest Kenneth,

When I was a little girl, I knew that someday I would get married. I guess when we are young and life is less complicated, we assume these things will "just happen." As I grew older and entered into relationships, though, I learned many lessons. There was a lot of heartache and self-realization involved in searching for "the right" person.

The night you and I met, all of my questions about who is the right person for me were answered. I remember how long we talked and laughed, how you looked at me with your beautiful brown eyes and smiled your beautiful smile. Even before our first embrace, I already felt the comfort and security of your arms around me . . . what a wonderful feeling! I felt so close to you immediately and knew you were sincere and caring. It was that very night that I knew we would be together forever.

I guess that brings us to this moment. We have done so much planning over the last several months and it hasn't been easy. Our road ahead will be difficult at times, but our love is so strong that I know that we are able to face all that our future holds for us.

I hope you know that from this moment on, I will love you for the rest of my life. I hope that we will always strive to communicate the way we do today . . . in our busy lives it has been one of the most important factors in our relationship. I need you to know I trust you completely and know that you will never be dishonest. Know that you will always be able to trust me. I would never hurt you or do anything to cause harm to the beauty we have found.

We have the elements of a strong relationship, and it begins with our unconditional love for one another along with honesty, trust, respect, and communication. They are also the elements of a strong family. God willing we are blessed enough to have a family and teach this to our children.

Kenneth, I have loved you for my entire life and was just waiting for you to find me. You are the true love I have always dreamed about. I love you so much that I cannot imagine my life without you. I have never been as happy as I am this very moment. I want you to know that if today were the last day of my life, I would have lived completely just having known you and felt your love.

Thank you for shedding your light on my life.

I love you,
Judith

In this chapter we'll look at communication, a second key element in finding an answer to the question, "Is this the person for me?"

TIME

On a Sunday evening after Thanksgiving I invited four couples to join me for dinner at a local restaurant following our weekly 5:10 p.m. young-adults Mass.

Three of the couples had married recently and the other would wed in a few months. All were in their late twenties or early thirties. The group included four lawyers, a special education teacher, a nurse, the administrative assistant of a business office, and a golf professional working at an area country club.

The purpose of this gathering was to discuss ideas for my homily at all the forthcoming Christmas Masses. They knew in advance that the basic questions for our discussion would be: "What are some of the major concerns for people in today's world? What are yours? How do these connect with the Christmas message?" Two of the couples were familiar with this experience, having participated the year before in a similar dinner dialogue.

In this two-hour, free-flowing exchange, one word emerged summarizing what they considered to be a universal and crucial challenge—time, or better, the lack of time in their lives.

Michael and Patricia, whose letters in the Introduction began this book, thought that after marriage they would have more time for each other. Unfortunately, because of their demanding schedules, their moments together even now in married life seemed minimal.

The engaged couple complained that previously they had fun whenever they met. Now, it appeared to them, every time they were together their time was spent struggling with practical details, or worse, family conflicts, about the imminent wedding.

All the couples expressed a common ideal that after children come, one of the parents would remain at home, but were unsure about how that could be done in our contemporary society with all of its financial pressures. The groom-to-be expressed his dilemma this way: "Do I abandon the work I love in the public sector as a prosecuting attorney for a better paying but more time-demanding position with a private law firm? My wife could then be home with our child, but will I ever be there to enjoy family life and to be the kind of father I want to be?"

While these were the time demands of relatively young, start-up couples, they observed that older married people share the same tensions. For them as well, life is too busy, time is at a premium, and moments of quiet togetherness are relatively rare, requiring a determined effort to arrange them.

TEN MINUTES A DAY

Therapist Alan Andrews would concur with the couples' consensus about the scarcity and preciousness of time. He is a major and popular presenter at Sunday afternoon marriage preparation programs sponsored by our Diocesan Family Life Office. Those sessions always attract thirty to fifty engaged couples, some of whom are there at my request.

Afterward couples tell me that Andrews immediately gained their attention by citing the fifty percent divorce rate of marriages. He next proposed a suggested practice guaranteed to insure marital success.

The therapist recommended that at the end of every day husband and wife sit down in a quiet space for ten minutes. One spouse initiates the experience by putting aside personal preoccupations, looking into the eyes of the other, and saying: "I love you very much. Tell me about your day." This partner then has five minutes to share the day's good and bad experiences.

The other next reciprocates in similar fashion: "I, too, love you very much. Now tell me about your own day." And for five minutes, the initiating spouse can likewise speak about the day's good and bad events.

If this procedure is to be successful, two words or concepts have to dominate the daily ten-minute exercise: time and communication. The married couple must make finding that quiet space and time a top priority in their always busy lives. They also, however, need the ability to communicate effectively in a loving and listening manner.

LISTENING

Persons with parents, relatives, or others close to them afflicted by Alzheimer's disease or serious dementia know how difficult, sad, and painful this situation can be. Caregivers in those cases face the unenviable task of guiding such individuals through hard choices that sometimes inflict a series of losses upon them. For example, the increasingly forgetful and confused ones, for their own safety and that of others, must give up driving a car. Later they usually need to abandon home or apartment for an institution that can provide the necessary assistance and supervision. Eventually, these afflicted persons may require yet another transfer to a still more skilled nursing facility.

These steps or moves do not happen easily. All involved experience moments of sadness and anger, family arguments and harsh exchanges, grief and depression.

The Notebook, Nicholas Sparks' best-selling novel, dramatizes these kind of anguished struggles. The beginning two-thirds of the book is an intriguing, clever, and touching love story; the concluding third recounts the end years for Noah and Allie, a couple married nearly a half-century.

There were signs of deterioration in Allie. "An iron in the freezer, clothes in the dishwasher, books in the oven. . . . But the day I found her in the car three blocks away crying over the steering wheel because she couldn't find her way home was the first day I was really frightened."

Her husband took her to Dr. Barnwell for tests and consultation. The physician finally pronounced his devastating diagnosis. "I'm so sorry to have to tell you this . . . but you seem to be in the early stages of Alzheimer's. . . ."

Allie and Noah decided to marshal all their resources so they could live out those final days together at the Creekside Extended Care Facility. Over the next several years Noah cared for his spouse with great tenderness, watching her memory gradually decline, seeing her slip into another world, and waiting for those miracles, those miraculous intervals when Allie temporarily recovered, recognized him, and knew who he, she, and they were.

Their four decades of married life had sharpened Noah's communication skills. He had gained an ability to pick up what Allie was thinking and feeling from her nonverbal gestures. "Our life together," he observed, "has enabled me to see the clues, even if she does not know them herself."

In one of those rare but brief miracle periods of recognition, his wife reveals how couples who communicate well, as they had, need not always use words to connect. Allie tells Noah, "Don't try to say anything. . . . Let's just feel the moment."

Noah understands well that spouses can lovingly listen to each other and powerfully communicate in silence.

> We sit silently and watch the world around us. This has taken us a lifetime to learn. It seems only the old are able to sit next to one another and not say anything and still feel content. The young, brash, and impatient must always break the silence. It is a waste, for silence is pure. Silence is holy. It draws people together because only those who are comfortable with each other can sit without speaking.[1]

Effective communication among couples begins by listening with love. One pays attention to the other, seeking to catch the other's thoughts or feelings being expressed by words or actions, in verbal or nonverbal ways.

That requires a forgetfulness of self, setting aside one's own worries or preoccupations and concentrating on the other. This is a clear illustration of the self-giving love described in the previous chapter.

The communication continues when the listener tries to reflect back in her or his own words the content and feelings expressed by the other. When that has been successfully accomplished, the speaker will possess a satisfying sense of being heard and understood.

In the ten-minute daily exercise outlined above, the listener, after five minutes, turns speaker and the speaker becomes the listener.

BUILDING COMMUNICATION SKILLS

At the end of my initial interview with an engaged couple, I ask them to complete FOCCUS. FOCCUS, an acronym for Facilitating Open Couple Communication, Understanding, and Study, has been designed by Sister Barbara Markey and is distributed through the Omaha Diocesan Family Life Office which she directs.

Each couple answers the almost two hundred questions separately, marking on the answer sheet "agree," "disagree," or "uncertain" for every inquiry. There are additional questions for those in interfaith relationships, a second marriage, or cohabiting situations.

After the couple completes this process, our receptionist uses the companion software to enter their answers and produce for them a twelve-page computerized printout, including graphs of the dozen areas covered by the FOCCUS exercise.

When I describe at the start of our interview the FOCCUS project awaiting them at the conclusion of their first visit, the couple usually seems intrigued by the concept and anxious to get at it. The exercise caused an immediate explosion with one couple. She rushed through the questions, swiftly marking "agree" or "disagree" after each inquiry. He, on the contrary, required much longer and often penciled in "uncertain."

In the cab of his truck afterward, the bride-to-be expressed her annoyance with both the length of time he took and the numerous uncertain answers he gave.

The FOCCUS experience actually revealed something profound about their personalities and a deep difference in the way they approach issues. An awareness of those differences and a resolution of them will be critical, if they are to enjoy a satisfying and successful marriage.

She is a quick decision-maker; he is a ponderer, a man who weighs matters carefully before making judgments. Neither style is right or wrong, good or bad, but will nevertheless probably at times prove irksome to the other.

Imagine this couple leaving the home en route to purchasing a new vehicle. We could conjecture that at the first dealership she immediately declares, "I want the red car over there in the parking lot." He remains silent for awhile, then carefully studies the window sticker listing the cost and at last cautiously responds, "I think we should visit a few other places and compare their prices or examine their specials."

It would not be surprising for this couple, after years of marriage and many such clashes over major and minor matters, to discover that she has slightly slowed down her decision-making and he has speeded up his own process of making decisions.

Another couple, in their thirties and the second marriage for him, found after FOCCUS that they had neglected talking about money. Both had secure jobs and substantial salaries. The possibility of conflict over financial concerns appeared very remote. Yet money matters rank high on the list of potential danger areas for spouses.

Engaged couples almost always label FOCCUS a test. "How did we do on the test?" "When do we get to take the test?" FOCCUS, however, is not a test, cannot predict marital bliss or misery, and does not indicate whether a couple should marry or separate. It has been constructed simply to facilitate communication between the prospective bride and groom. After conducting the FOCCUS experience with hundreds of engaged couples in recent years, I would judge that FOCCUS is most successful in achieving this more limited and realistic goal.

DISCERNING THE REAL THING

In the last chapter, school counselor Rosalie Brennan proposed ten questions to assist individuals and couples in discerning if their friendship and love is the real thing. She poses the following series to aid individuals and couples in discovering if their communication is also the real thing.

1. Do you both really communicate and listen to each other?
2. Does your partner know what makes you happy, sad, or angry?
3. Are your problem-solving styles similar or complementary?
4. How do you resolve conflicts—by avoidance, confrontation, or compromise?
5. Would you consider yourselves on the same intellectual level?
6. Have you common feelings about children and how to raise them?
7. Is your life assuming a new dimension in which you speak more about "our" time and "our" weekend, instead of "my" time and "my" weekend?
8. When you look at each other, can you guess (fairly accurately) how each other is feeling?
9. Does time go faster when you are together and slower when you are apart?
10. Do you share common interests?

SPEAKING OUT PROPERLY

In an earlier book, I repeated the lengthy and almost poetic hopes and expectations which Patrick penned about his approaching marriage to Christine. He began his letter with a description of their early dinner dates.

On those occasions, she automatically would take her fork and eat something off his plate. Having grown up with four brothers, he was accustomed to protecting the food on his plate and not letting someone take from it. While annoyed a bit by Christine's regular practice, he did not clearly surface that anger and instead resorted to various defensive measures—barricading his plate with water glasses, bottles, or the salt and pepper shakers. None of these worked.

One evening his annoyance broke through and he sharply asked Christine to stop. Driving home that night, she sat very quietly, and Patrick knew that he had hurt her.

The matter was not resolved, nor the distance over this issue lessened, until a month later. Then, on a business trip away and having dinner alone, Patrick observed an older couple at the table next to him. When their meals were served, the wife took her fork, as Christine would do, and reached for his plate. The husband, however, instead of resisting this move, held out his own plate so she could more easily take a portion of his dinner.

Patrick was deeply moved by that event and now better understood that Christine was "trying to teach me how to share."

The incident has a happy ending. Patrick went on to complete his hopes and expectations with a magnificently-worded and heart-warming list of future occasions when he hoped that Chris would be eating off his plate.[2]

Later, while reflecting on this letter, I realized that in the early stages of their courtship, the couple's communication skills were badly in need of improvement.

Patrick did not from the start adequately surface his annoyance at her actions. As a result, in a subsequent weak and unguarded moment, he inappropriately lashed out and hurt Christine. She, on the other hand, did not pay sufficient attention in the beginning to his irritation and, when hurt, retreated in silence. Both, apparently, left the conflict unresolved for perhaps a month.

Good communication requires listening with love, but also speaking out properly. Given our flawed human condition, no one does either perfectly. Those failures to communicate can hurt your beloved. Moreover, the closer you are to that person, the deeper and more serious the wound. Those situations demand that the individuals involved possess soft hearts, inner spirits very ready to seek and grant forgiveness. We will address this third key element in relationships now.

CHAPTER 3

FORGIVENESS

Tom attended Catholic schools in an east coast city from first grade through his senior year. After graduation he sampled several colleges and a few job opportunities, but kept returning to an occupation that began for him when he was eighteen—bartender. Tom finds the income is excellent and the work steady. And he rather enjoys his role as amateur priest/counselor/psychiatrist.

Jane's parents split when she was a very young girl. After the divorce, her mother moved to a west coast area where there were some relatives nearby. Jane accompanied her mother, but during the summer months, regularly returned east and spent time with her father.

On one of those vacation visits, Jane, now in her late teens, met Tom at a bar with several friends. They quickly bonded and fell in love, and, Jane became pregnant early in the courtship. This unplanned development obviously complicated their lives. It also generated mixed reactions from her father on one coast, her mother on the other, and Tom's parents living in that eastern city.

What to do? They both rejected abortion. Jane could, of course, leave Tom, go back with her mother, and have the baby there. But the two of them discarded that alternative because of their desire to work through this together. His parents, while troubled by the situation, nevertheless offered Jane and Tom space in their home. The couple finally decided that this was the best solution and accepted his parents' invitation.

Jane and Tom lived there for a few months, then purchased a house in an older but attractive section of the city. A short time later, Jane, who had been christened Catholic but never raised as one, began on her own a course in that faith. She was eventually received into full communion with the Catholic church, had the baby baptized, and during the Christmas holiday season accepted Tom's marriage proposal.

This couple, with a large group of family and friends, had made reservations for a huge party on New Year's Eve at a local hotel. Tom spoke in advance with the DJ and the hotel staff about his plan to propose just before midnight. At precisely 11:45 p.m. the DJ played the couple's favorite song, had a spotlight focused on Jane in the audience, and asked the stunned young woman to come forward. There, before two thousand revelers, Tom got down on bended knee, proposed to her, and presented his now weeping bride-to-be with a sparkling diamond. The onlookers roared their approval.

The journey of this couple to the altar followed a path filled with many potholes and frequent stumbling blocks. But they had both learned much through these difficulties and had overcome substantial obstacles. Now they felt ready for marriage. Why?

"When things are going well," Tom observed, "we are the happiest couple in the world. But we do have our sharp disagreements. I am like my father, quiet and wanting to be always under control. Jane, on the other hand, is much more emotional, and when upset, sails into me. That in turn raises my temperature and we have a pretty good spat."

Jane added, "Usually, on those occasions, we decide to go out for an hour's walk or a short dinner and let things cool down. Sometimes, however, there may be a few days of distance, of not saying much to the other, especially when it involves a major issue we cannot seem to resolve."

One of those serious conflicts occurred around the time when they booked the church for their wedding. Jane and Tom had made plans to cross the country by plane and spend some desirable as well as needed days with her mother. Tom had arranged coverage at the bar, and Jane was excited about a reunion with her mom.

Regrettably, Tom's employer notified him at the last minute that he couldn't give Tom the promised time off because a conflict had arisen. Jane was disappointed, hurt, and angered by this development. Tom did not like the turn of events either, but felt he had no choice. He needed the job and they needed the money.

This painful dispute did not destroy their relationship, but it certainly placed a strain upon both of them, reminding each that patience, acceptance, and forgiveness are essential elements of a successful marriage.

In this chapter we'll look at the dynamics of forgiveness, another key aspect of any successful relationship.

A STORY OF FORGIVENESS

Nearly a century ago, the musical *Show Boat* opened on Broadway to critical acclaim and enthusiastic audiences. Today, talented touring companies move from city to city in the United States with an updated presentation of this classic show. They, too, receive rave reviews and perform in sold-out theaters. The timeless story offers us an insight into the role of forgiveness in a relationship.

If our bright and musically talented teenage receptionist is any criterion, many young people, including those of you reading this book, will not know the story or recognize the songs familiar to and beloved by older folk. Youthful persons, however, should recognize the racial issues which form the backdrop of *Show Boat's* story. You can also relate to the relationship complexities that are central to the plot of this musical. A century ago legalized segregation existed in the deep South along "Ol' Man River," the Mississippi, the site of *Show Boat*. While the reality of segregation may be familiar, an understanding of miscegenation may be less so. It is the marriage or cohabitation of one person with an individual of another race, including and especially in the South, a white individual with a black individual. This marital or sexual mixing of races was culturally unacceptable then and, in some areas, legally prohibited.

The complex love affair which is the unifying thread linking together various elements of *Show Boat* still resonates today. At the beginning of the musical, young, protected, naive Magnolia, daughter of the river boat's owner, instantly falls in love with Ravenal, a wandering "river rat," a polished, charming gambler of questionable moral integrity. He, it seems, is equally infatuated with her, and they marry, much to the distress of Magnolia's mother.

Ravenal and his bride move to Chicago where he soon wins a huge amount in some gambling venture. With this abundance of money they transfer from a small, inexpensive apartment to the posh Palmer House hotel. Unfortunately, Ravenal's restless heart and addictive habit lead him on to continued wagers. Eventually his fortune changes and he loses all.

Magnolia struggles with the deteriorating lifestyle, yet defends her husband before everyone. However, Magnolia's world soon collapses. Ravenal sends a note by messenger to his wife indicating that there is nothing left to pawn or money to pay bills. He encloses enough cash for Magnolia to return home and tells her of his enduring love, but in view of the failures decides that he must leave her. Ravenal, unaware that his wife is pregnant with their first child, disappears totally from the scene.

Magnolia is devastated, near despair. But close friends, recognizing her musical and acting talents, find work for Magnolia in a Chicago nightclub. She instantly becomes a star and twenty years later, considering retirement, rejoices that her grown daughter possesses similar gifts and will soon replace her on stage.

In the show's final scenes, Ravenal reappears, full of regret and guilt. "I'm so sorry," he mutters to a companion. Ravenal is stunned when he realizes that the young woman, this emerging star, is his own daughter. Magnolia then sees Ravenal and, after hesitation, runs into his arms and embraces him.

One, bitterly remorseful, begs forgiveness; the other, still deeply in love with her husband, swiftly grants it. *Show Boat* ends with that relationship of Magnolia and Ravenal, once so idyllic, then bruised and broken, now restored. Their bond is now different, but deeper, with the ugly wound healed, but a permanent scar remaining.

FLAWED HUMANITY

Show Boat is, in a sense, a tragic-comedy. At the end, the central characters are reunited and emerge victorious over the darkness surrounding their lives. But a heavy tone or atmosphere of misery permeates the musical. The refrain "Tired of living, but scared of dying" in "Ol' Man River" repeatedly fills the theater. So, too, the lives of its characters are often crossed with sorrows and tragedies. But life, like the massive river, inexorably rolls on.

Tom and Jane certainly can relate to those positive and negative dimensions of life. Some of their burdens were or are beyond their control (the divorce of her parents and the demands of his employer). Some, however, arose from their own free choices (the pre-marital sexual activity and the unexpected pregnancy). But with love and determination they have worked through many of these serious challenges. They are, at times, "the happiest couple in the world." But, at other times, they do have "sharp disagreements."

Both the musical *Show Boat* and the lives of this couple underscore a critical truth: All human beings are flawed. No one loves perfectly; no one communicates perfectly; neither does anyone forgive perfectly.

We should never be surprised by this fact. Still, we continue to be hurt, troubled, or even disillusioned when we encounter instances of our flawed humanity, whether within ourselves or in others. Personal experience, Christ's example and preaching, St. Paul's words, observations from contemporary authors, and teachings of the Catholic church all testify to the reality of our flawed humanity.

PERSONAL EXPERIENCE

Is there anyone who at a single sitting consumes just the right amount of peanuts, popcorn, or potato chips?

How often have we made resolutions on New Year's Eve or for Lent and never fully carried them out?

Are there moments when we regretfully mutter to ourselves: Why did I say that? Why didn't I say this? Why did I do that? Why didn't I do this?

Do you know individuals with serious addictions? Have you witnessed how, for example, alcohol, drugs, or gambling can enslave them? Only a persistent, day-by-day effort will enable them to reshape their lives in the face of these weaknesses.

CHRIST'S EXAMPLE AND PREACHING

In the garden of Gethsemane, Jesus felt deeply troubled and full of sorrow. He took three of his closest followers with him and asked them to sit nearby while he prayed. Later Christ came back to the three, looking for support and comfort. Instead, he found them sound asleep.

His comments of disappointment teach us much: "So you could not keep watch with me for one hour? Watch and pray that you may not undergo the test. The spirit is willing, but the flesh is weak" (Mt 26:40-41).

St. Paul's Words

In chapter seven of his letter to the Romans, St. Paul speaks about the conflict within us, about the flesh and the spirit, about the battle between good and evil going on inside every human being.

"The willing is ready at hand," he says, "but doing the good is not. For I do not do the good I want, but I do the evil I do not want."

At the end of this chapter, St. Paul laments: "Miserable one that I am! Who will deliver me from this mortal body? Thanks be to God through Jesus Christ our Lord" (Rom 7:18-19, 24-25).

Observations From Contemporary Authors

Some reviewers judge that Canadian theologian Ronald Rolheiser has written one of the best books on spirituality in the past decade. *The Holy Longing: The Search for a Christian Spirituality* begins with an insightful and sharp description of our inner, and, consequently, our outer restlessness. We have such strong desires, he maintains, that we are "forever restless, dissatisfied, frustrated, and aching."

Citing both classic scholars like Freud and Jung as well as modern commentators who speak of running with wolves or fire in the belly, Rolheiser summarizes these notions in this way:

> Whatever the expression, everyone is ultimately talking about the same thing—an unquenchable fire, a restlessness, a longing, a disquiet, a hunger, a loneliness, a gnawing nostalgia, a wildness that cannot be tamed, a congenital all-embracing ache that lies at the center of human experience and is the ultimate force that drives everything else. This dis-ease is universal. Desire gives no exemptions.[1]

Judith Viorst, graduate of the Washington Psychoanalytic Institute and a popular writer, wrote *Necessary Losses* in 1986, a book that remained on the *New York Times* bestseller list for six months. She maintains in it that to grow we must give up certain myths, let go of some false expectations, understand there are necessary losses in our lives.

More specifically, as examples, we need to face these inescapable truths:

- In other people and in ourselves there is a mingling of love with hate, of the good with the bad.
- There are flaws in every human connection.
- Hurts cannot always be kissed and made better.
- "Our dreams of ideal relationships" must yield to the imperfect connections.[2]

THE TEACHINGS OF OUR CHURCH

The familiar biblical account of Adam and Eve in the Garden of Eden as recorded in the book of Genesis begins with a caption, "The Fall of Man" (Gen 3). The Catholic church terms those bad, poor, wrong choices of our ancestors as the original sin. Sin occurs when we fail to follow the divine imperative or God's voice in our hearts. Adam and Eve committed sin by violating the Creator's prohibition about the tree of life in the middle of the garden.

We call their sin the "original" sin for several reasons: it was a sin of our ancestors, those from whom we trace our origin; it was the first or "original" sin; it was and is the source of all subsequent sins.

There were several consequences of this original sin: shame and guilt entered the world. They "realized that they were naked." They "hid themselves from the Lord God among the trees of the garden." Our ancestors' relationship with God was broken and death became their destiny. The Creator banished them from the garden and placed an angel, a cherubim with a fiery revolving sword, to guard the way or entrance to that garden and the tree of life. Adam and Eve as well as all subsequent men and women began to experience conflict, stress, and struggles. Human beings and most animals no longer peacefully coexist. Childbearing now involves pangs of pain. We earn a livelihood through fatiguing hard work and by the sweat of our brows.

As a result of original sin, humanity needed a savior who could correct our flawed condition. Christ did this by his dying and rising. Through baptism we share in that saving action of the Lord. The baptismal font's water washes away sin, makes us members of a Christian family, brings the risen Jesus into our hearts, and opens the gates of heaven.

But baptism does not eliminate the inner turmoil, the dis-ease of desire, the turbulence our weak and disordered human nature causes. Only by God's amazing, healing grace can we rise above those compulsive tendencies within us.

It takes a lifetime of human struggle and divine grace to overcome these effects of original sin. Because of our weakened condition we do hurt others and others hurt us. The next section will explore ways of reducing those hurts and healing the wounds that arise from them.[3]

MANAGING CONFLICTS AND HEALING HURTS

Standing before the altar in their formal wedding attire, both bride and groom look angelic and saintly. But appearances, as you know, can be deceiving. Your own courtship experience—often an extended one in today's world—has undoubtedly helped you understand that you are neither angels nor saints.

You genuinely care for each other and share idealistic dreams of the future. Nevertheless, you both recognize your flawed, weak natures and, at least theoretically, expect conflicts or misunderstandings with each other.

Moreover, you hear and accept the admonition that there will be dark and difficult days in your future.

Your verbal promises express these expectations and recognitions. You vow to be true to each other, to love and honor the other in good times and in bad, in sickness and in health, for better, for worse, for richer, for poorer all the days of your life until death do you part.

How, in a practical way, you can manage the conflicts and heal the resulting hurts will be the thrust of this particular section. The degree to which you can do this will help you know the "rightness" of your relationship.

1. UNDERSTAND AND ACCEPT EACH OTHER'S FAULTS AND SHORTCOMINGS.

In the first chapter it was noted, among the characteristics of love, that it "respects." Love takes people as they are, not as they should be or as we may want them to be.

Expecting a major change, improvement, or conquest of a major fault, significant shortcoming, or irritating habit will only lead to disillusionment. We can grow. We do overcome some of our weaknesses. The married couple may even experience a gradual diminishing of certain behavioral patterns that irk one another.

In general, however, the shift must come in their attitudes, not in their actions, in their hearts, rather than in their habits. Instead of seeking for a change in the other, successful married couples inwardly become more accepting of one another's faults or shortcomings. They rather unconsciously concentrate on the positive qualities which drew them together in the first place and which continue to sustain their love.

2. WISELY MANAGE CONFLICTS.

Jack Lawyer earned his M.B.A. from the University of Michigan and worked quite successfully for many years as a leader in the corporate business world. He then turned his training, expertise, and experience to the task of improving communication among people rather than of increasing profits for a company.

For twenty years he has been conducting communication skill-building seminars and workshops for a wide variety of organizations throughout the United States. These sessions deal with, among other topics, reflective listening, problem solving, and conflict management. The first item, reflective listening, is the essential element in addressing issues which involve problems and conflicts. That type of listening was discussed in Chapter Two.

The diagrams which follow illustrate both the development of a conflict and a process for managing or even resolving the dispute. The application to a basic disagreement or strong argument between spouses should be evident.

Normal, Non-conflicted Situation

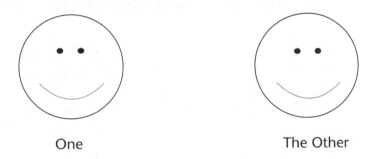

One   The Other

In this situation, the emotions are relatively still, communication is on a conversational level, and discussions flow easily.

Beginning stages of a conflict

One   The Other

Something one has done or not done, said or did not say irks, angers, or even hurts the other. The other's temperature rises and, depending upon the circumstances, may reach or exceed the boiling point. The one senses a distance, a frown, a turbulence, but is not certain about the nature of the difficulty and feels slightly uneasy.

Developed conflict condition

One   The Other

The other, finally, in verbal or nonverbal ways, in pointed hints or frontal attack, surfaces the irk, anger, or hurt. That raises the temperature of the one who may respond with defensive or even hostile comments. The negative emotional levels of both continue to elevate and a battle ensues.

Start of a solution

One   The Other

At some point, the one recognizes the futility of this confrontation, remembers the importance of reflective listening in such a condition and tries to override her or his negative emotion by being truly attentive to the other's message. This effort may feel forced at the start and carry a sarcastic tone in the beginning. But it can produce a slight diminishing of negative emotions in the other.

Continued diffusing of the conflict

One   The Other

As the one continues to listen reflectively, both temperatures further drop and root issues may surface.

Solving the problem or managing the conflict

One   The Other

With the emotions at safer low levels, the one may now tentatively take a turn to speak, but must do so wisely. The one's attention will be to define differences, state similarities, and address concerns. If at any point, the other's temperature starts to rise a bit, the one ceases to speak and returns to the listening mode.

Conflict managed

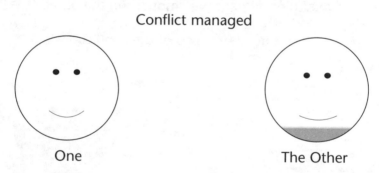

One   The Other

At this point, both recognize that a currently unresolvable issue exists, leaving a certain distance between them and a layer of negative emotion beneath the surface. But the separating issue and emotional negativity are manageable. The plus factors in their marital relationship override the existing separation and sublimated emotion.

Problem solved

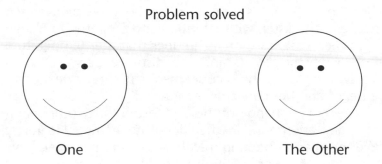

One   The Other

Sometimes the confrontation surfaces on issues or concerns, especially when they involve mere misunderstanding or poor communication, that can be resolved in a manner that is quite satisfactory to both. They then return to that relatively still, conversational, and easy dialoguing state. In fact, their marital bond is probably tighter and their relationship warmer as a result of this whole process.[4]

Ralph and Elaine, married nearly forty years, have two children and, to their delight, recently became grandparents for the first time. The pattern of their confrontations illustrate these principles.

When Elaine feels irked, angered, and hurt, often by something omitted rather than committed, her temperature rises, but she does not articulate the difficulty for a period of time. A certain distance develops in the relationship and Elaine ponders the right time to express her annoyed feelings to Ralph.

Ralph is Irish, peace-loving, and conflict-hating. He senses the gap between them and begins to feel some negative emotions, dreading the anticipated disruption of his serenity.

When Elaine finally finds the appropriate time and speaks with strong feelings about her concerns, it automatically raises Ralph's temperature. He blasts back with a few negative, maybe even sarcastic, remarks, further elevating her negative feelings. But within a very short time,

Ralph fights back his temper, rises above his own anger, and begins to listen with attention and empathy to Elaine.

In their case, as soon as he does that, her temperature immediately plummets and the distance between them dissolves. As far as she is concerned, she simply needed to be heard and her concerns recognized.

A recent exchange of this sort lasted for two hours on a Sunday afternoon. In their lengthy married life rarely have they had a shouting match. And seldom, if ever, have they gone to bed without the surfaced issues being resolved or at least managed.

3. SWIFTLY FORGIVE AND SEEK FORGIVENESS.

One of the signs that a person is falling in love is an increase in willingness to be vulnerable. An individual begins to share with the other deeper feelings, inner anxieties, and generally well camouflaged uncertainties. That may be true more often for the man than for the woman.

In doing so, self-revealers disclose soft spots in their being, places in their personality where they are especially vulnerable, sensitive areas around which they can easily be hurt or wounded.

Thus, in many ways no one can hurt another as a husband may wound his wife or a wife her husband. Given our flawed nature, that will happen. When it does, it can cut deeply and leave an open sore. For that reason, married persons need to forgive swiftly and swiftly seek forgiveness.

"I am sorry" will do the trick. So will "I apologize." But the best expression, more personal, more profound, more vulnerable, is "Please forgive me." That acknowledgment of full responsibility for a hurt encourages the wounded one to accept totally the other person.

Swift forgiveness and reconciliation heals the open wound, although sometimes, in major matters, the scar will remain forever.

Ralph and Elaine rarely, if ever, allow their confrontations to carry over through the next day or days. Tom and Jane, whose example opened this chapter, on the other hand, as a younger couple, seem at least on occasion to need a few days for the thorny matter to settle and their troubled feelings to subside.

MODELS OF FORGIVENESS

It helps to hear of others who had hearts that swiftly and completely forgave, even in the most trying of circumstances.

MALE HEROES

Jesus. Christ was totally innocent and without sin. Moreover, he spent the three years of his adult life simply going about doing good. Yet envious opponents criticized him, plotted his death, and falsely accused him. In addition, among his closest followers and friends, one betrayed him, one denied him, and the rest ran away.

Still, while hanging on the cross in excruciating agony for three hours, Jesus spoke words of forgiveness for all his persecutors: "Father, forgive them, they know not what they do" (Lk 23:34).

Lawrence Jenco. On January 8, 1984, Father Lawrence Jenco, program director for Catholic Relief Services in Beirut, Lebanon, was roughly kidnapped by terrorists. They abducted him, mistaking him for another U.S. government official. For five hundred and sixty-four days, Jenco, who came to that country to serve its poor, endured severe beatings and cruel confinement, despite his age and poor health. He had, therefore, real reasons for bitterness.

Just prior to Father Jenco's release, one of his guards, Sayeed, who had at times brutalized him, sat down on a mat next the priest. He said to the still blindfolded clergyman, "Abouna (Arabic meaning dear father), do you forgive me?"

Jenco later reflected on the experience: "These quietly spoken words overwhelmed me. As I sat blindfolded, unable to see the man who had been my enemy, I understood I was called to forgive, to let go of revenge, retaliation, and vindictiveness."

He remembered his reply, "Sayeed, there were times I hated you. I was filled with anger and revenge for what you did to me and my brothers. But Jesus said on a mountaintop that I was not to hate you. I was to love you. Sayeed, I need to ask God's forgiveness and yours."

Shortly thereafter, released and flown to Rome, he stepped from a car in that city as a reporter shouted at him from a distance, "Father Jenco, what are your feelings toward the terrorists who held you?"

Without much thought, Lawrence Jenco responded, "I'm a Christian. I must forgive them."[5]

Pope John Paul II. Two pictures, several years apart, but both wired around the world, dramatize the spirit of forgiveness exemplified by Pope John Paul II.

The first photo captures the hand of a would-be assassin holding a gun firing down on the Holy Father as he moved away from a mob of pilgrims at St. Peter's Square in Rome.

The second picture, months after the pope's recovery from those bullet wounds, catches Pope John Paul II in white cassock and skull cap sitting across from his assailant in a Roman jail and holding both his hands.

The words spoken were not disclosed, but the photographed scene clearly expressed remarkable forgiveness and reconciliation.

Joseph Cardinal Bernardin. In the mid 1990s this cardinal archbishop of Chicago struggled twice with cancer. The first, in the pancreas, led to surgery which rendered him "cancer free" for fifteen months. The second, in the liver, eventually claimed his life in 1996.

Painful and trying as were these two episodes with cancer, they could not compare with the extreme agony and deep humiliation of another dark experience. A young man named Steven Cook, very ill with AIDS, accused Cardinal Bernardin of sexually abusing him years earlier while Cook was a seminarian in Cincinnati.

One hundred days passed before the false charges were resolved. It appeared that Steven Cook was a pawn in a wider plot. Enemies of the cardinal, a New Jersey lawyer specializing in suing the clergy for sexual abuse, an immature therapist unskilled in hypnotism, and an eager media combined to draw Cook into this evil web. Several months after the accusation, Cook, on his own initiative, asked a federal court judge in Cincinnati to drop the charges.

From the beginning, Cardinal Bernardin sensed that Cook might be an unwilling or unknowing partner in this scheme. He prayed for him. He also wrote a note of concern to Cook, a letter never delivered to him by his lawyer. This note read, in part:

> As I thought it over, I began to think that you must be suffering a great deal. The thought came to me yesterday morning that it would be a good thing if I visited with you personally. The purpose of the visit would be strictly pastoral—to show my concern for you and to pray with you. If you are interested in such a visit, please let me know. I will come to you if you wish.

After the case was dropped, the cardinal resumed his busy schedule. But he often thought of Cook in his lonely, illness-ridden exile and judged that the experience of the false accusation would not be complete until he met and reconciled with Cook.

Through Cook's mother, Cardinal Bernardin made contact with him and learned that the unfortunate young man also had a real desire to meet with the cardinal.

They did so at a neutral, private location, St. Charles Borromeo Seminary in Philadelphia. Cardinal Bernardin describes in detail this very moving reconciliation experience in his book, *The Gift of Peace*. Before separating, Cook said to the cardinal, "A big burden has been lifted from me today. I feel healed and very much at peace."

On the airplane returning to Chicago, Cardinal Bernardin remarked that he "felt the lightness of spirit that an afternoon of grace brings to one's life."

Later, the two dying persons, one from cancer, the other from AIDS, connected occasionally through letters and phone calls. Cook died before the cardinal, but now fully reconciled with the church and his family. On his deathbed, Steven Cook turned to his mother, smiled, and said about his return to the sacraments of the church, "This is my gift to you."[6]

FEMALE HEROES

While these are indeed four inspiring stories of forgiveness, they all involve men and, for the most part, people in official religious positions. Here are some similar examples of forgiving women.

Magnolia. Earlier in this chapter I summarized *Show Boat* and its final reconciliation scene between the fictional Magnolia and her long-absent husband Ravenal. He begged her forgiveness; she, after momentary hesitation, granted it fully and totally.

Maria Goretti. This young Italian girl was born at the turn of the last century into a poor farming family. After her father died when she was ten, Maria assumed the responsibility of caring for four little brothers and their neighbors' children while area adults cultivated the fields.

One of the workers, an eighteen-year-old named Alexander Serenelli, became inflamed with passion for Maria, not yet twelve, but physically mature. He several times tried to seduce her, but she always refused. Finally, in his rage over the refusals, he stabbed Maria fourteen times. She died a day later, but only after expressing forgiveness for her assassin.

The court convicted Alexander and sentenced him to thirty years in prison. He was a surly and unrepentant prisoner until his eighth year in jail. One night he dreamed that Maria appeared to him, presenting her murderer with a bouquet of flowers.

His heart changed instantly. Upon his release from prison eighteen years later, he first went to Maria's mother and begged her forgiveness, subsequently receiving communion with her at Christmas Mass.

Three decades after that, sixty-six-year-old Alexander Serenelli knelt in St. Peter's Square beside Maria's mother and two hundred and fifty thousand other people as Pope Pius XII canonized Maria, declaring her to be Saint Maria Goretti.[7]

Mary Ehrlichmann. On a Sunday night, Donald Ehrlichmann and his son Michael, nineteen, picked up three hitchhikers in north Minneapolis, three young men seemingly in need of a friend. Almost immediately one pulled out a pistol and demanded their wallets. Father and son handed them over, then Donald deliberately swerved the car into a tree. The crash dazed Michael sitting in the front seat. The father pried open the car door and ran, yelling to divert the hikers' attention from his son. The pistol-bearing robber shot him three times.

More than nine hundred people came to the Lutheran church for the father's funeral. They heard one son, a ministerial student, ask for their friends' and society's forgiveness of the three who murdered his father.

In the evening, after the burial, Mrs. Ehrlichmann wanted to tell the three unapprehended young men they were welcome in her home, if this was the kind of love they could understand and need. She finally wrote an "Open Letter to the Three Boys Who Murdered My Husband":

> During the past three days my grief and desolation have been eased and comforted, by the love and faith of so many wonderful friends and relatives. But, in the midst of all this, and especially in the quiet moments, my thoughts keep turning to you three. You may feel that you are men, but to me you are just boys—like my own sons—and I wonder to

whom you are turning for comfort and strength and reassurance.

I suppose I will never know what motivated your actions that night, but if the shots were fired out of sheer panic, my heart aches for you and I wish there were only some way I could help you in what you must be suffering now.

If hate made you pull that trigger, I can only pray that you can come to know the love of God that fills the heart and leaves no room for hate. If you were under the influence of drugs, please, for my sake and your own, don't waste your lives, too. Get help and rid yourselves of that stuff.

Please, if you see this, find a church some place where you can be alone; then read this again. Know that God forgives you and that my family and I forgive you—then go out and make something worthwhile out of the rest of your lives.

God keep and bless you.[8]

Marlene Rosales. Lazaro and Marlene Rosales graduated from medical school in the Philippines. Subsequently, they came separately to Meriden, Connecticut, for their internships at a hospital in that city. It was there they met, and it was there that two months later Lazaro proposed.

In June 2000 they celebrated their silver wedding anniversary and, according to Filipino tradition, did so with a splendid public celebration. There was a solemn nuptial Mass with renewal of vows, impressive music, attendants in formal attire, and a reception at the nearby hotel for hundreds of guests.

Have they enjoyed a perfect relationship for twenty-five years? No. Their personal quirks drive each other mad. For example, he won't ask for directions and she sometimes demands too much at once.

Do they fight? Yes.

But they hold hands in public and say every day, "I love you."

Are they committed? Of course. Marlene comments, "You tend to think only of how to make it last, how to make it work."

Making it work naturally includes seeking and granting forgiveness when the quirks get out of hand or when they do have a fight.[9]

DISCERNING THE REAL THING

School counselor Rosalie Brennan returns now with another series of ten questions to help individuals and couples discern if the forgiveness element in their relationship is the real thing:

1. Can you say "I am sorry" when you have made a mistake or hurt the other person?
2. Are the other's parents still married?
3. What kind of a marriage do the other's parents have?
4. How do the other's parents treat one another?
5. Does your partner have a deep faith and practice that faith?
6. How committed is each one to making the marriage work?
7. Does she/he have a sense of humor?
8. Can your partner laugh at herself/himself?
9. Whose needs does the other think of first in the relationship, or about life in general?
10. Are you comfortable holding hands in public?

A FINAL WORD ABOUT FORGIVENESS

The first chapter on friendship concluded with some words from Henri Nouwen on the effort involved in sustaining and strengthening friendships. We conclude this chapter and Part One with insights also from Father

Nouwen about broken relationships and the forgiveness needed to heal them.

That gifted and now deceased author observes:

> I am deeply convinced that most human suffering comes from broken relationships. Anger, jealousy, resentment, and feelings of rejection all find their source in conflict between people who yearn for unity, community, and a deep sense of belonging.

Nouwen suggests forgiveness as a remedy for broken relationships: "By claiming the Holy Trinity as home for our relational lives, we claim the truth that God gives us what we most desire and offers us the grace to forgive each other for not being perfect in love."[10]

QUESTIONS FOR REFLECTION

If you have pondered the general question "Is this really love?" as well as the specific one, "Is this the person for me?" and have read through these pages about friendship, communication, and forgiveness, you may now want to reflect upon the following summary questions. They may help you to make wise decisions in these critical matters.

1. Is the other person your best friend?
2. Do you attempt to meet the other's needs before you take care of yourself?
3. Do you really communicate and listen to each other?
4. Do you share common interests?
5. Can you say you are sorry when you have made a mistake or hurt the other person?
6. How committed is each one to making the relationship (and eventual marriage) work?
7. Are you more giving or less giving to others because of this relationship?
8. Do you pray better and more often since this relationship started?
9. Have you found your joys doubled and sorrows diminished as a result of the relationship?

PART TWO
SHOULD WE LIVE TOGETHER FIRST?

CHAPTER 4
FACTS

Terry and Nora met at medical school, where she was a year ahead of him. Their paths crossed often at classes and a number of mutual friends tried to match them up, but the proposed connections never seemed to work out.

Both were regular churchgoers, had been active participants in religious services prior to medical school, and now usually attended the same Mass each Sunday night.

On one of those evenings, Terry, a basically shy person but feeling attracted to Nora, came to church in a sour mood. He was annoyed that one of those "arranged" connections with her did not materialize. The reason: he had suddenly been called out of town on an emergency.

At the greeting of peace during the liturgy, he turned to those nearby and to his surprise discovered Nora standing in the pew immediately behind him. There was a smile and a handshake. After the service, she, equally drawn to him, walked slowly away from church hoping he would overtake her. Because of his diffident nature, Terry thought instead that she was running from him.

Both lived in a large high-rise set of apartments two blocks from the church. Nora made her way there alone feeling sad and judging that Terry was not interested.

Back in her apartment she fretted for a while, then decided to take matters in her own hands and called him. "Hi. This is Nora. Strange coincidence that we just met at church, right? Would you like to go out for ice cream?" Terry's heart skipped several beats, but he blurted out his acceptance and drove her to an ice cream parlor for dessert.

A year later they became engaged and set the date for their wedding. Two months prior to the wedding Terry moved in with Nora. They did so reluctantly, concerned about their parents' reactions and troubled by the moral and religious implications of this cohabitation. But their motivation seemed almost totally financial.

Both Nora and her female roommate had at that time recently graduated from medical school. The partner immediately returned home, leaving Nora alone with payments on a relatively large two-bedroom apartment. Meanwhile, Terry's lease on his own quarters was due. Since Terry and Nora were strapped for cash and shortly would be married, the idea of renewing his long-term lease for only a few weeks' use seemed highly impractical. Consequently, they decided it was best for him to move into her apartment.

The move placed an added strain on a personal commitment they had made to each other—abstaining from sexual intercourse until marriage. However, the two-bedroom apartment made that goal at least feasible, even though the arrangement presented a further challenge to the ideal they had set for themselves.

Just a generation ago, Terry and Nora's decision to move in together would have been much more controversial. Today, it is their wish to abstain from intercourse until marriage that makes them unusual. But the choice to live together is often taken for granted. After all, "lots of people do it."

Today, over fifty percent of engaged couples would, like Nora and Terry, answer yes to the question, "Should we live together first?" In a relatively short period of time, the number of couples living together has grown in quantum leaps, making that practice a commonplace occurrence. They are living together and, for various reasons, judge that cohabiting before marriage is best for them. One of the reasons often given is that it is a way of finding out if a couple is well suited and ready for marriage. But is that really true? In this chapter we will look at what contemporary researchers are discovering about cohabitation and how it seriously calls such an assumption into question. But first, we need to define the terms cohabitating and cohabitation.

The research to be cited generally defines cohabitation as a couple who have been living together at least four nights a week for an extended period of time in which there is a certain commitment to each other and a recognition that together they form, in some sense, a "family."[1]

THE SITUATION IN THE 1980S

In the United States during the 1980s there was a remarkable increase in cohabitation. It was a commonly-accepted concept bolstered by supportive sociological research.

A remarkable increase. The number of unmarried couples living together in 1984 totaled 1,988,000—a tripling since 1970. That represented four percent of all couples or family units residing in the United States. However, only one out of four to one out of eight cohabiting couples eventually married. This tenuousness of the living together arrangement had and has a critical impact which we will describe in the next chapter.

An accepted concept. That "common sense" notion dominated informal discussions and permeated the media.

Contemporary commentator Dr. Joyce Brothers summarized and expressed this concept which advocates of cohabitation regularly cited in defense of their position. "I wouldn't dream of marrying someone I hadn't lived with. That's like buying shoes you haven't tried on."

The *New York Times* ran a full-page ad for one popular national magazine which featured a smiling young woman making these observations:

> "I still can't believe it. . . . Jeff and I are married! We eloped last week . . . and I'm weak with joy! A lot of our friends say why get married? . . . Why not just live together? We did that and the time comes when you have such a deepening friendship and such a commitment to each other you want to spend your lives together officially. . . ."

Supportive sociological research. Several surveys conducted in the 1970s and carried over into the 1980s suggested that cohabitation effectively sifted out incompatible couples, served as a training and adjustment period, improved mate selection, and enhanced the chances of avoiding divorce. Moreover, other research uncovered little evidence that living-together couples had more difficulty remaining married than those who had not lived together prior to marriage.

These three potent factors made very awkward and difficult the task of those who argued that cohabitation was both morally wrong and an unwise way to prepare for marriage.

A SHIFT IN THE 1990S

Research in the 1990s reported information that reversed the sociological findings of the 1980s and seriously questioned the "common sense" argument. While the number of couples living together at the time of their marriage preparation continued to increase (now at almost 50%), studies revealed a decline in attitudes toward marriage itself, a higher risk of divorce for cohabitating couples and less satisfactory adjustments once married for those couples who lived together beforehand.[2]

Decline in attitudes toward marriage. Fewer persons are choosing to marry today. From 1975 to 1995, the number of U.S. marriages declined twenty-five percent. Catholic Church figures listed in 1974: 406,908 marriages; in 1995: 305,385 marriages.

Moreover, as noted earlier, a high percentage of cohabiting couples never marry. With couples cohabiting for the first time, only fifty-three percent marry. With those cohabiting for the second and third time, but ten to thirty percent marry. Moreover, thirty percent of cohabitating couples intend never to marry at all.

Higher risk of divorce. Cohabitors who do marry are more at risk for subsequent divorce than those who did not cohabit before marriage. In the United States the risk of divorce is fifty percent higher for cohabitors than for non-cohabitors. The divorce rate is even higher with previously married cohabitors and serial cohabitors (those who have had several cohabitating experiences). There are some indications that the divorce rate is higher for couples who live together for a longer period of time, especially over three years.

Less satisfactory adjustments in marriage. Cohabitors generally report lower satisfaction with marriage after they marry than do noncohabitors. There are indications that some living-together couples have more problematic, lower-quality relationships with more individual and couple problems than noncohabitors.

ENTERING THE 2000S

As we entered the new millennium more recent studies and contemporary observations confirmed the continued rapid increase in the number of cohabiting couples.

In a *USA Today* cover story (April 18, 2000), the headline states: "Changing the shape of the American family." A subheading goes on to announce: "No longer undercover, living together is replacing marriage." An illustration above the cover story includes a graph of this shift. "The number of unmarried couples cohabiting continues to increase. 1960: 439,000; 1998: 4.2 million (Source: Census Bureau)."[3]

However, in addition to underscoring a continued decline in the attitude toward marriage and the negative impact that living together has upon the process of preparing for marriage, the research and observations surfaced a new and also worrisome phenomenon: the harmful effect of cohabitation upon children.

Continued decline in attitude toward marriage. As an example, the *USA Today* story cited above tells about Sarah Abbot, twenty-four, of San Francisco who has lived with Daniel Price for about eighteen months. Her mom's divorce has scared her. "I want to be sure, and I think either subconsciously or not, it affects the way I look at marriage. It is not a huge priority in my life now."

She probably will marry Daniel sometime and definitely would if she were to have a child. However, for now it is for Sarah, "no big deal. I can really only go on how it has worked for me. I am surprised how well it is working. I wouldn't want to do it any other way."

Negative impact of living together upon the marriage preparation process. In that same *USA Today* article, University of Chicago sociologist Linda Waite reports in her book *The Case for Marriage* that studies indicate how living together can undermine marriage. "Cohabiting changes attitudes to a more individualistic, less relationship-oriented viewpoint. She finds that "live-ins are less happy than marrieds, less sexually faithful and less financially well-off."

Dr. Laura Schlessinger, whose written words and radio talks seem to generate either intense love or bitter hostility, penned a column appearing on April 2, 2000 in a local newspaper entitled, "Living together as trial run for marriage fails on many levels."[4]

She cites several research articles and reports on the negative impact of cohabitation. Women in cohabiting unions, Dr. Schlessinger notes, are more than twice as likely to be the victims of domestic violence than married women. They also have rates of depression more than three times higher than married women and more than twice as high as other unmarried women. Cohabiting couples also have higher divorce rates and more infidelity by both partners.

Harmful effect of cohabitation upon children. Dr. Schlessinger also is particularly concerned about the harmful effect of cohabitation, divorce, and poor marital relationships upon the children involved. She cites a British study which found the incidence of child abuse was "an astounding thirty-three times higher when the mother was cohabiting with a boyfriend unrelated to her children. Even when the live-in boyfriend was the father of one or more of her children, abuse was still ten times more likely." Her book, *Parenthood by Proxy: Don't Have Them If You Won't Raise Them* treats this topic at length.[5]

The National Marriage Project is a nonpartisan, nonsectarian and interdisciplinary initiative supported by private foundations and affiliated with Rutgers, the State University of New Jersey. In January, 1999 David Popenoe and Barbara Dafoe Whitehead completed, as part of this project, a comprehensive review of recent research entitled, "Should We Live Together: What Young Adults need to know about Cohabitation before Marriage." That massive paper with forty-seven footnotes, documents all the statistical trends noted in this chapter, but also discusses in some detail the pejorative impact of cohabitation upon children.[6] Consider these ominous facts:

- In 1997, thirty-six percent of unmarried-couple households included a child under eighteen.
- Nearly half of all children today will spend some time before they are sixteen in a cohabiting family.
- Three quarters of children born to cohabiting parents will see their parents split up before they reach age sixteen, whereas only a third of children born to married parents will suffer that same fate.
- Fewer cohabiting mothers now go on to eventually marry the child's father.
- Children currently living with a mother and her unmarried partner have significantly more behavior problems and lower academic performance than children from intact families.
- The great majority of children in unmarried-couple households were born from a previous union of one of the adult partners. This means that they are living with an unmarried stepfather or mother's boyfriend with whom the economic and social relationships are often tenuous.
- American studies about child abuse in cohabiting couples are not satisfactory. Nevertheless, research in Great Britain reports that children living with cohabiting, but unmarried biological parents are twenty times more likely to be subject to child abuse.

Needless to say, these statistics portray the dreadfully harmful impact of cohabitation upon children.

Sarah Abbot, scarred by her mother's divorce, moved in with David "to be sure" that a future marriage with him would work. Apparently the research statistics were unknown to her or at least did not alarm Sarah. Or, she may have dismissed them and, instead, praised the words of Larry Bumpass, a University of Wisconsin-Madison demographer and sociologist. Bumpass has reported similar negative effects of cohabitation, but cautions that all these statistics do not mean doom for every cohabiting couple. "Statistics," he insists, "are about averages, not the experience of any one particular person."

LEARNING FROM EXPERIENCE

Marsha, a twenty-two-year-old graduate student, had fears similar to those of Sarah Abbot. Her parents divorced when she was seven. She moved in with Tom to test the relationship and to make sure she wasn't jumping into marriage. The young woman details her experience and what she learned from it.

My own parents divorced fifteen years ago, so I was determined not to jump into marriage. That's why I moved in with Tom—so we could develop our relationship and get to know each other first.

It went from beautiful to miserable in about four months. I was knocking myself out to please him, feeling insecure whenever the arrangement seemed the least bit shaky. And I was using sex in a way that was false to myself. Intercourse was my way of reiterating, "The relationship is still on," of asking, "Is the relationship still on?" It was my way of saying, "Keep me, I'm good!" (even when sex wasn't always that good), and of reassuring myself, "See, he still loves me."

Important questions were never settled, things such as: "What if I get offered a good job in another state?" or "What if he decides to go back to school?" or "The pill is making me depressed—should I stop taking it?" We'd just end up in bed again, without resolving things. I got to the point where I felt like yelling, "Sex, schmex! I just want you to talk to me!"

I told Tom I wanted to move out and think things over. I wanted him to really see me and hear me as a person—something our sexual involvement made it hard for him to do. I wanted perspective—and friendship.

I must say that after the initial shock Tom rose to the challenge. We spent a whole year getting to know each other every way but horizontally. We must have logged a thousand hours just talking. And I knew I wasn't sliding into something through compliance and neediness and emotional fuzziness: I was exercising real sexual intelligence. That gave me new respect for myself—and for Tom.

We're getting married. It took a while, but now we know we're committed.[7]

These are dry but hard facts. What do they mean? In the next chapter we will reflect on that statistical data and other research, seeking to draw some general conclusions about living together before marriage.

Chapter 5

REFLECTIONS

John and Rose Ann each wrote letters describing their hopes and expectations about the future. Here are Rose Ann's words to John that the priest read during their wedding service:

> Over the last six years you have become my best friend, my confidant, my passion, my strength. I remember the day we met. You were dating one of my best friends. I came to her dorm room to borrow something. You were sitting at her desk. I'm not quite sure why I remembered that. We became good friends that year and spent that entire summer together. My friends teased me when I tried to explain that we were "just friends," and I scolded them when they referred to you as my boyfriend. Just because we spent all of our time together, at the movies, the drive-in, restaurants, and then there were all those hours spent on the phone.
>
> I guess they saw what it took us a year to figure out. We just worked well together, we fit like two puzzle pieces. We complement each other in every way. When I'm stubborn, you're patient, when I'm uptight,

you're relaxed. You know when I'm happy and when I'm sad, and vice versa.

I remember the night I realized we were so much more than "just friends." We were at the drive-in. I don't remember what either of us was wearing or what the weather was like or even what movie we saw. The one thing I remember about that night is our hands. They were resting on the center console. If they had been any closer they would have been touching. There was a nervousness in the air. I could feel the heat from your hand, but they never touched. I remember that as the night we almost held hands. It was one of the best nights of my life.

I knew for years before you proposed that I wanted to spend my life with you. We've seen our share of good times and bad over the years. I look forward to all the good times our future will bring. Anniversaries, the birth of our children, proms, and graduations. Also all of the little things like watching you search the kitchen for your keys when they're sitting on the counter, reading the Sunday paper together, seeing that look of triumph on your face because you made the green light, and holding your hand. And I know together we can conquer all the bad.

When I was about sixteen my father told me that I would marry someone just like him. Of course at the time I cringed at the thought. It brings me great comfort today knowing he was right, knowing that you possess all of the qualities I loved about him.

You are kind and gentle. You give of yourself freely and never ask for anything in return. I know if I asked you to, you would try to move heaven and earth for me. I admire your strength and generosity and the way you look at everything as if for the first time. I feel safe and secure when you are near me. I feel like part of me is missing when we're apart. I love you with all of my heart. I can't wait to start building our life together.

John and Rose Ann had met as students in a small, Catholic liberal arts college. His major was marketing and hers was psychology. After graduation he obtained employment in sales with a Washington, D.C., home improvement company. She continued her studies back home. In time the firm sent him to Atlanta, where eventually he became manager of its branch office there.

Soon they purchased a house in the suburbs, and she moved south to join him several months prior to the wedding.

Here are John's hopes and expectations for their marriage:

When I first met Rose Ann we got along great with one another and became very good friends. Over time we became more than friends and my life was changed forever. You hear all the time that husbands and wives were best friends. We did everything though: went camping, went to drive-ins, talked 'til early hours of the morning, we loved spending time together. When we started dating we went through a lot with one another. Some good, some bad. I love her more every day because of those times. Sometimes I feel I say that I love her too much, but the love I feel for this woman is indescribable. She is everything I could ever want.

Over the years we have learned so much from one another. We know what the other one is thinking most of the time. I can tell her anything and know she would understand. We have a special bond that can never be broken. I would do anything for her without thinking. Her smile is what keeps me going all the time. Whenever we are apart that's all I have to think about

*to let me know everything is going to be all right. I
can't wait to have children together and watch them
grow. We are going to have a great life together. I don't
know where I would be today without you. I love you
always and forever.*

John and Rose Ann's story puts a very human face on
the question of living together before marriage. It's a
romantic story, to be sure, and as already noted, many people today wouldn't be overly concerned about their living
together before marriage. But in light of everything that
we've seen thus far in this book, the question remains: Is
such cohabitation before marrying the best way to prepare
for a future as spouses and parents? Let's keep John and
Rose Ann in mind as we look at the sociological trends,
some insights from practical experience, and the wisdom of
the church on the question, "Should we live together first?"

THE INSIGHTS OF
SOCIOLOGICAL STUDIES

Studies of cohabiting couples provide more than statistics; they offer a picture of trends and concerns. They shed
light on issues that a couple who has been living together
before marriage should be aware of as possible areas of
concern for them in their married life. They also provide
couples who are thinking about living together with good
reasons for caution.

Studies cited in the previous pages indicate that in general, as an average, living together before marriage is not the
best preparation for a marital union. Why not? I will seek to
offer some answers to that question or at least provide a few
reflections upon this topic in the discussion that follows.

A repeated word of caution here: as Dr. Bumpass
observed in the last chapter, we will again be looking at

general principles, statistical averages, and common trends. They do not necessarily spell doom for each couple or mean that all married persons will experience every negative effect of cohabitation. Nevertheless, what are these downside impacts of cohabitation on marriage preparation?

Couples who live together before marriage are less committed to the institution of marriage and more accepting of divorce. Consequently, they are more likely to seek divorce as the solution to problems and issues as they arise which challenge the marriage.[1]

Sexual fidelity is less in the marriage of cohabitors than it is in the marriage of non-cohabitors. A woman who cohabits prior to marriage is 3.3 times more likely to be sexually unfaithful than a woman who had not cohabited before marriage.

Cohabitation promotes an excessive individualism. Married persons generally value interdependence and the exchange of resources. Cohabitors generally value independence and economic equality. Moving into marriage does not automatically change those values.

Those living together sometimes marry because of pressure from their families or the pressure to provide a stable home for children. While these may be desirable goals in themselves, they are not adequate reasons for a marriage, nor do they guarantee a successful marital union.

Cohabiting couples tend to develop unreasonably lofty expectations of marriage. When the realities of married life—with its challenges and disappointments, its richer and poorer, sickness and health, better and worse moments—puncture their dream world of married togetherness, they can grow disillusioned and disheartened.

Couples who live together before marriage often duck tough issues. They know or intuit that a majority or at least a high percentage of cohabiting couples split prior to marriage. Aware of the fragility of their relationship, they may avoid discussing or dealing with problematic areas lest those discussions weaken or break their already tenuous connection.

One scholar studied one hundred couples who had lived together, married, and within five years divorced. The majority had discussed only in the most general terms and infrequently, prior to the wedding, sensitive issues like finances, careers, leisure activities, and children.[2]

THE WISDOM OF PRACTICAL EXPERIENCES

As I mentioned in the Introduction, over the past decade I have had the opportunity to listen to some five hundred engaged couples talk about their relationship together, and often continued the conversation with them into their married lives. I've also talked with parents of young adults, counselors, and fellow priests over the years about the questions of couples living together before marriage. And in doing so, I've recognized that certain conclusions, often supported by psychological and sociological research, can be drawn from our collective experiences. I offer those here for your consideration.

Cohabiting couples frequently repress anger and avoid criticism of each other's annoying behavior. The fragile nature of the cohabiting relationship can make a couple extremely cautious and reluctant to complain about the other's insensitive or irritating actions.

Repressing anger in this fashion can only lead to disaster. Eventually it surfaces, frequently in explosive eruptions hurtful to both parties. Moreover, the couple may begin to view marriage as the miracle solution to their conflicts.

Sadly, countless couples would testify today that getting married does not produce a miraculous change. If anything, it surfaces negative habits which have been repressed during the courtship and which may gradually emerge with greater intensity as the ordinariness of marital life takes over.

The method of handling finances before marriage may not prove so satisfactory after marriage. As noted above from sociological studies, prior to the wedding couples treasure independence and economic equality. Solid marriages require, instead, interdependence and a mutual exchange of resources.

The free spending habits of one partner during cohabitation may be perfectly acceptable, even pleasing to the other. Once married, that may not be the case. Saving for a house, anticipating babies, and providing for their children's future college education now become more pressing issues. For the budget-conscious spouse, use of precious dollars by the other for unnecessary items or extravagant ventures will surely cause conflict.

Opposition to the cohabitation, especially from parents, close family members, or treasured friends, places a strain on the relationship. Most of us, at least to some extent, are people pleasers. To have people we care about, particularly our fathers and mothers, critical of our actions causes us pain. That in turn can impact the interaction between the cohabiting man and woman.

In an effort to avoid a confrontation, dishonesty, untruthfulness, and inauthenticity may creep into relationships with others, including and above all, parents. This, of course, applies mainly to those who are away from home and at some distance because of college or work situations. Rather than disappoint parents, incur criticism, or experience rejection, the cohabiting person fudges, conceals, or even lies about the cohabitation arrangement.

A person can never be deeply at peace or content when knowingly dishonest, untruthful, or inauthentic. Moreover, the truth eventually emerges and often with hurtful, even disastrous, results.

Some half-serious, half in jest, suggest that immediately before Parents Weekend on college campuses there is a flurry of activity around dormitories, a swift exchange of roommates, a quick (although generally temporary) return to the rooming situations dads and moms presume exist.

Violation of one's conscience or religious upbringing in this matter can produce an undercurrent of guilt. Whether slight or substantial, this guilt robs an individual of deeper serenity and peace.

Some years ago, writer Jimmy Breslin said, "Nobody leaves the Catholic church."[3] He meant that when you have been raised in the Catholic church—baptism, penance, communion, and confirmation—and for all your adolescent life have been taught its teachings, then you rarely are able simply and radically to discard the church or discount those instructions.

The cohabiting Catholic person, for example, may no longer participate at Sunday Mass on a regular basis and may openly reject the church's tenets as outdated. Yet the rejection or abandonment may not be as total or as permanent as it seems or sounds. This dynamic would be true of anyone raised in a religious tradition, regardless of the particular faith.

The Catholic church's teachings on premarital sex and cohabitation, which will be described shortly, are quite clear and serious. They penetrate our souls and inner being more deeply than we may realize. A certain undercurrent of guilt, however slight, can very possibly trouble the cohabiting persons who grew up as a Catholic or who has had similar moral or religious training in early years.

THE TEACHING OF THE CHURCH

The moral teachings of the Catholic church are usually generic and universal. For some, these norms seem restrictive, cold, and irrelevant. In their view, they limit the conscience of freedom, ignore the complexities of human existence and fail to keep up with changes in the modern society.

The fact is, however, that observing those rules liberates us, enriches our lives, and gives us clear guidance in today's confused world. The moral laws, often cast in negative terms, thus have a positive dimension to them.

For example, the commandment "You shall not kill" also means "You shall preserve human life." This precept, among other things, requires that we take care of our bodies, not abuse them. People who heed this commandment experience good health and inner peace; those who do not suffer ill health and interior turmoil.

Individuals who abuse alcohol are apt illustrations of these truths. Their out-of-control living eventually destroys their health and robs them of peace. Those who use alcohol in moderation, on the contrary, frequently find that it even improves health and deepens their joy.

The Trappist monks at the Abbey of the Genesee south of Rochester, New York, sing the psalms every day. I have been there for retreats more than a dozen times, and one phrase they chant lingers with me throughout the year: "Happy are those who keep God's law." That verse is based on Psalm 1, which describes the true happiness of one who does not follow the guidance of the wicked but delights in the law of the Lord.

All of this applies to the church's guidance on sexuality, which can actually liberate, enrich, and guide us. Here is a summary of the Catholic Church's main teachings about premarital sex and living together.

Sexual intercourse is a complex, explosive, and powerful action designed by God to express, sustain, and deepen the love between a husband and a wife. Sexual intercourse, within or outside marriage, normally creates an atmosphere of intimacy or closeness. Those struggling with low self-images, doubting their attractiveness to others, or suffering lonely moments in life may, usually in an unconscious way, find through sexual activity temporary relief from the struggle, the doubts, or the loneliness.

The immature adolescent, already buffeted by the struggling, doubting, and suffering which accompanies youth, who also must cope with difficult family tensions at home, likewise may find instant intimacy, comfort, and reassurance through intense genital stimulation or sexual intercourse. But older, insecure, and immature individuals also sometimes seek answers and reassurance in similar fashion.

One of the lead characters in *The Love Machine*, a popular 1960s novel, is fat little Ethel Evanski from Hamtramck, Michigan. Ethel had always wanted to be beautiful, even as a child. As a grown-up, she had perfect breasts and a splendid waist, but otherwise was not that attractive. Moreover, from early childhood she had been enamored with movie stars and public celebrities. Finally finding her way to New York and a clerical position in the media industry, she began to sleep with many men. However, Ethel's selections of sexual partners and her motives for these short-term liaisons were unhealthy.

"Ethel wouldn't settle for anything less than a top celebrity. A one-night stand with a celebrity was preferable to a mediocre existence with a nobody." When she held a movie star in her arms and he murmured his delight with her, "that moment made up for everything in the world. During that one moment she was beautiful—she was *someone*. She could forget who she was. . . ."

In one of those encounters, Ethel made love to the president of the television network (IBC). Despite his drunken condition, the man likewise praised her sexual prowess. As he did so, "she forgot that tomorrow he would pass her in the hall without a nod. Right now she was making love to the president of IBC. And right now she *felt* beautiful. . . ."[4]

These experiences made her feel, for the moment, important, loved, and significant. But the next morning they were gone, and she was left with even deeper and darker doubts about her own self-worth.

Unfortunately, movies and television dramas convey this message of pure pleasure and immediate intimacy without portraying the complex nature of sexual intercourse. For example, the film *Autumn in New York* (2000) conveys the truly inspirational message about an extremely self-centered older man transformed through the darkness of loss into, at the end, a loving person feeding his infant grandchild. But in the early part of that movie, this man meets and is mesmerized by a younger woman, and she with him. They sleep together the very first night. It all seems so natural, so flawless, so uncomplicated. Later some of the complexities and questions arising from this immediate coupling do slightly surface. However, the impression given, as is often the case on the screen, is that sexual intercourse follows instantly, wonderfully, and simply after a man and woman discover an attraction for each other.

Reality is quite different. Apart from the risk of a deadly disease or unplanned pregnancy, casual sex profoundly impacts the emotional lives of its participants. Complex questions arise: Was it a single night fling? Did she use me? Does he care? Will this last? Am I the only one?

Without permanent commitments, these anxious and often painful inquiries continue.

The sexual drive is not only *complex*, it is also very *explosive*. In Rose Ann's letter at the beginning of this chapter, she mentioned the night at a drive-in when their long-time friendship shifted into a romantic relationship.

> The one thing I remember about that night is our hands. They were resting on the center console. If they had been any closer they would have been touching. There was a nervousness in the air. I could feel the heat from your hand, but they never touched. I remember that as the night we almost held hands. It was one of the best nights of my life.

The Creator made our drives or hungers for food and sex very powerful. One pushes us to eat and thus remain alive as a person. The other drives us to copulate and thus reproduce so that the human race will survive. Because the sexual drive is so explosive, our culture and church have rules and traditions which, if followed, help channel this potent force in positive directions.

Sexual intercourse is, finally, *a powerful action that expresses, sustains and deepens the love between husband and wife.* Therapist Martin Helldorfer has written about the unique and remarkable power of sexual intercourse to unite individuals and its ability to express mutually the inner feelings of those so joined.

He likens this experience to a city that has several narrow streets and is experiencing a day in which gentle breezes surround the area. Those hardly noticeable movements of wind, when gathered and tunneled through the narrowed passages of that city, attain an intensity otherwise unknown.

In his analogy, sexual intercourse may:

> . . . channel the hardly noticeable movements within and between persons to a point of intensity that is as inescapable and unavoidable as are the tunneled winds of city streets. Intercourse has a way of highlighting and bringing to consciousness all that is harmonious as well as conflictual in a relationship. That is why feelings of love and hate, fullness and emptiness, joy and sadness, anticipation and disinterestedness break in upon the act of intercourse in such astounding and unplanned ways. The act intensifies and magnifies what otherwise might be unobserved. Ecstasy or depression following the physical expression of love are but an indication of the harmony and disharmony within and between persons.[5]

Husbands and wives have through their vows exchanged a total gift of themselves to each other. Sexual intercourse can, as Helldorfer writes, uniquely and remarkably express that union, sustain it during difficult periods, and continually deepen the relationship.

From the *Catechism of the Catholic Church*:

> Holy Scripture affirms that man and woman were cre-
> ated for one another. . . . "Therefore a man leaves his
> father and his mother and cleaves to his wife, and
> they become one flesh." The Lord himself shows that
> this signifies an unbreakable union of their two lives
> by recalling what the plan of the Creator had been
> "in the beginning": "So they are no longer two, but
> one flesh."[6]

Every act of sexual intercourse is meant to be open to the wonder-filled possibility of a man and a woman creating with God new human life. Couples sometimes wish to return to the priest and to the place of their marriage for the baptism of their children, especially their first. Having served as a parish priest in the same basic area for twenty years and officiated at several hundred weddings in those churches, this has often been for me a joyful experience. I was with them at the sacred altar when they vowed their mutual love until death; I am now with them at the baptismal font celebrating this miracle of life which they, with God, have brought into this world.

At the homily during the rite of baptism, I pose this question to the parents: "When your child first came forth and you held or gazed at this baby, how did you feel?" These are the typical answers I hear: "Overwhelmed; ecstatic; can't believe it; joyful; filled with love; deeply grateful; proud; in the presence of a miracle." At the baptism of an eleven-pound, six-ounce girl, the father respond-ed the he had felt very proud; the mother answered that she had felt very relieved!

But a miracle it is. Every child conceived is a coopera-tive venture between the parents and the Creator. We might say that father and mother create the body, and God directly creates the soul. That soul—spiritual, immaterial, immortal—gives life to the result of their union, and requires the hand of an all-powerful God for its creation.

High school girls who have had sex: 1999—below 50%.

College freshmen who accept this statement: "If two people realize they like each other, it's all right for them to have sex even if they've known each other for a very short time": 1987—52%; 1999—40%.

Teens who have had sex and wished that they had waited longer: 2000—66%.

Teens who say that sex is not acceptable for teenagers: 2000—60%.

Teens who believe that society should give teenagers a strong message that they should abstain at least until they are out of high school: 2000—93%.

Despite movies, television dramas, and novels, America's adolescents apparently understand better today the complex, serious, and unique dimensions of sexual intercourse.

From the *Catechism*:

Those who are engaged to marry . . . should see in this time of testing a discovery of mutual respect, an apprenticeship in fidelity, and the hope of receiving one another from God. They should reserve for marriage the expressions of affection that belong to married love.[9]

Cohabitation poorly prepares couples for marriage, places them in precarious moral situations, and indirectly undermines society's regard for family life. The sociological surveys and actual experiences cited in this and the previous chapter provide strong support for the statement that, in general, as a rule, or for most couples, living together prepares them poorly for marriage.

Moreover, if one accepts the moral teaching that sexual intercourse must occur only within marriage, cohabitation places any couple in a precarious situation making observance of that code of conduct extremely difficult.

Terry and Nora, whose story introduced this section on living together, had separate bedrooms in their apartment. For the few weeks remaining prior to the wedding, that arrangement made their goal of virginity before marriage at least feasible, even though surely much more challenging.

John and Rose Ann, whose story began this chapter, discovered that their friendship had blossomed into romance at a drive-in when their hands almost touched. The energy, the nervousness, the powerful attraction between them, part of God's plan drawing a man and woman together, obviously led to some lovemaking later on. Given their living together in that new home for several months prior to the church service, it would seem likely that sexual intercourse had become a part of their lives before the nuptial vows.

Living together also indirectly and subtly undermines society's regard for marriage and family life. Cohabiting couples display all the appearances of a married pair. Then, they may ask, why marry at all? In addition, the question of the impact upon the welfare of any children involved seems rarely to be raised—whether about children who might be born from this relationship or children connected with one or both of the partners from a previous relationship.

Surveys reveal an increasing number of younger people who decide they will not marry ever, and simply go on living together. *Time* magazine's cover story for its August 28, 2000, issue carried these captions: "Who Needs a Husband?" and "More women are saying no to marriage and embracing the single life. Are they happy?" Headlines in the article itself declared: "More women are deciding that marriage is not inevitable, that they can lead a fulfilling life as a single."

A survey in the essay reported on a study that asked: Would you consider raising a child on your own? The "Yes" response: single women—61%; single men—55%.[10]

The negative impact upon our society's view of marriage through such an increase in cohabitation over recent years is complex, somewhat obvious and yet subtle as well. The effect will not be fully grasped for decades.

From the *Catechism*:

> In a so-called *free union*, a man and a woman refuse to give juridical and public form to a liaison involving sexual intimacy. . . . The expression covers a number of different situations: concubinage, rejection of marriage as such, or inability to make long-term commitments. All these situations offend against the dignity of marriage; they destroy the very idea of the family; they weaken the sense of fidelity. They are contrary to the moral law. The sexual act must take place exclusively within marriage. . . .[12]

The sacrament of matrimony assures the couple of Christ's life-long presence in their marriage providing guidance and strength at all times. The popular, but controversial practice of using a unity candle as part of the wedding ritual dramatizes this presence of the risen Christ in a couple's married life. As they light and hold the candle between them, it visually reminds the bride and the groom, as well as the attending guests, of Jesus' part in their marriage, of the Lord's promised, future assistance for the couple, and of Christ as the light of the world.

For those who are baptized, this light of Christ first began to dwell within each one (symbolized then by a candle) when the priest or deacon poured blessed water and pronounced potent words.

The wedding ritual reminds us that the same Lord's providence brought them together. Now, before the altar, as they exchange vows and minister the sacrament to one another, Jesus cements their relationship until death do they part. Christ the light also promises that he will walk with them all the days of their lives. As their companion, this Lord of light promises to give them needed guidance when they are in doubt and adequate strength when they are in darkness.

Each year on their anniversary, we encourage couples to light their candle, watch the video, glance at the photographs, reread their hopes and expectations (if they selected that option), and recall Jesus' promise to be by their side always. The closer they are to one another, the closer they will be to God; the closer they are to God, the closer they will be to one another.

From the *Catechism*:

> The grace proper to the sacrament of Matrimony is intended to perfect the couple's love and to strengthen their indissoluble unity. . . . Christ dwells with them, gives them the strength to take up their crosses and so follow him, to rise again after they have fallen, to forgive one another, to bear one another's burdens, to "be subject to one another out of reverence for Christ," and to love one another with supernatural, tender, and fruitful love.[13]

Having examined at some length and depth the phenomenon of living together, I now offer a few practical suggestions for couples who are in love and contemplating marriage.

CHAPTER 6

GUIDELINES

Anne and John grew up in the same area of central Michigan but did not meet until they both began college. The two of them fell in love while at Michigan State. He pursued a degree as a packaging engineer, and she sought a diploma in art history.

Their relationship developed and they began to plan their marriage, but Anne needed first to secure a master's degree, if she hoped to find future employment in that field. Fortunately, an opportunity for the advanced study materialized at a large university in the east.

What to do?

She accepted the offer and moved to that eastern city; John then found a job with International Paper that both utilized his education and enabled him to live near Anne's university. They rented an apartment between his job and her school, moved in together, and reserved a church for the wedding scheduled about a year later.

Anne was initially quite nervous when they met with the priest to arrange details. Her sister back home had been turned down by the local pastor when she sought to marry in their parish church because she was living with her fiancé. Anne feared a similar response, but that was not the case.

In the ensuing months Anne and John attended Mass quite regularly, participated in the diocesan marriage preparation program, and planned details of the wedding ceremony.

Following marriage and graduation with her master's degree, she found employment on the west coast, and John transferred to another company near San Francisco. How do they feel now, several years later, about living together before marriage while she completed her studies? They judge that for them it was the right thing to do.

But what about other couples, like yourselves? Are there suggestions for persons in love who either are living together or are contemplating that move? This chapter will offer some guidelines for them.

COUPLES AND THEIR PARENTS

During a recent Christmas holiday season, two male college students sat in front of me on an Amtrak train heading into New York City. Alone, but occupying seats on opposite sides of the aisle, they chatted back and forth about a variety of topics. The youthful travelers spoke so loudly that their neighbors could not help but overhear snippets of the conversation.

The discussions touched upon, among other things, church and synagogue (one was Catholic, the other Jewish), life after death, and, of course, girlfriends. Both recounted their most recent experience of staying overnight at the houses of those young women.

One fellow told of sleeping by himself in a downstairs bedroom. He noted the presence of an active "baby monitor" in the room and wondered if her parents wanted to be certain that there were no secretive, middle of the night activities between this visitor and their daughter.

The other fellow responded that his girlfriend's parents did not seem to care whether the two of them slept together or not. His tone of voice and comments indicated a certain disappointment in that parental attitude, almost a wish that they were stricter about this matter, more like the parents of his companion on the train.

The rather amusing conversation between these colleagues introduces our examination of this issue—cohabiting couples and their parents. However, it also highlights the real distinction between premarital intercourse and living together. These practices are not identical, although obviously quite connected.

Studies indicate that 90% of engaged couples are sexually active before marriage; on the other hand, only 50% are living together. Many couples, therefore, clearly are engaging in sexual intercourse, yet are not living together. Moreover, as we have seen, some engaged couples, although presumably not a high percentage, are living together but abstaining from sexual relations prior to marriage.

There are, consequently, two issues before us: premarital chastity and living together. Here, however, we treat only the question of living together.

The decision to live together or to continue living together necessarily influences the relationship of the couple to both sets of parents. What will our parents say? Do they approve? How will our decision and their attitudes affect our connection with them? Will the relationship we have with one another be impacted by what our parents say or do about living together? Has it already been impacted?

In responding to those questions, couples struggling with this issue—and statistics indicate that a majority of engaged couples or couples quite serious about each other are indeed pondering the matter—should find the following information helpful.

This lengthy section contains nine typical suggestions which have been offered to parents who likewise are struggling with the issue of their cohabiting or potentially cohabiting children. They may have read these words or heard these guidelines. As you look through the following pages, imagine your parents reading them or listening to a presentation containing these points. That process could help you understand, as the contemporary saying goes, "where your parents are coming from." This in turn may facilitate a dialogue with them on this matter.

Begin early. When a living-together engaged couple arrive at the parish office to arrange a wedding, it is almost too late to address this issue. True enough, if cohabiting pairs openly admit their status, the clergy need to respond. But the teaching of truth and forming of attitude must happen much earlier—at the high school and early college level. Wise, firm and loving parents are the best instructors for this task.

A college friend of mine at Yale came from New Jersey, growing up with strong parents who possessed that kind of wisdom, firmness and love. In the 1950s, the challenge for parents and young people was not premarital sex or living together, but attending Sunday Mass. I remember vividly he and his siblings remarking that this was not even a debatable matter in their house. You simply went to church and were expected to go. That parental direction was not dictatorial or unenlightened; it was merely a mother and father clearly communicating and firmly implementing an essential value and practice.

While living together is a more complicated matter and contemporary society is much different, still that same type of parental wisdom, firmness, and love applied to this issue is much needed. To achieve success with such a goal, however, parents must know the facts.

Know the facts. The two previous chapters identified from serious sociological studies and popular presentations many reasons why cohabitation fails as the best preparation for marriage.

If parents have a clear grasp of these facts, they will be able in an informed and non-defensive manner to guide their teenage and early twenties children. That type of ongoing instruction may sow lasting seeds in the hearts and minds of their adolescent offspring at quiet moments long before they face even the thought of moving in with someone. Then, later, when a partner or the culture suggests this as an alternative possibility, the wisely and well-guided daughter or son will possess some well-founded and deeply ingrained objections to that proposal.

Listen. When the existing or perhaps about to happen cohabitation becomes known to the parents and a discussion about it arises with daughter or son, the initial dialogue will very often be filled with a very high level of feelings.

The parents may feel hurt, disappointed or angry. The daughter or son will likely seem nervous, defensive, or even hostile.

As long as the intense feelings dominate, it is very difficult—in fact nearly impossible—for the truth to penetrate, for reason to rule, and for both parties to reach an acceptable agreement.

It is, therefore, critical for the older and presumably more mature parents to rise above their negative feelings and to listen with great love and attention to their child and possibly her or his beloved. We might describe the ideal procedure in this way: Hear what they have to say. Ask for their reasons why they now are or do contemplate living together. Catch their feelings. Then recast in your own words what you have heard and observed, communicating this message, without judgment or criticism, back to them.

That process accomplishes several objectives: it lowers the emotional level; it builds trust within the younger pair; it makes a rational dialogue feasible. The listening will also reveal, often in a surprising way, the reasons why the couple judge that living together is a desirable step for them.

Once the couple feel they have been truly heard by the parents, dad and mom can respond with their own thoughts and feelings. In this response, the facts mentioned above should be helpful and can counter some of the arguments or reasons proposed by the couple.

It is unlikely that this initial dialogue will resolve the conflict or result in total agreement. But it can reduce tensions, clarify issues, and open avenues for future discussions.

Disclose convictions and feelings. At the end of the initial conversation or soon at a subsequent dialogue, parents need to state softly, but with clarity and firmness their convictions about cohabitation. In addition, they would do well to communicate how they feel about their daughter or son moving in with this person.

Children need to know that cohabitation will cause pain, sadness, or hurt to their parents. They may still proceed as planned, but at least they will understand their parent's convictions and how their own actions can prompt these negative feelings within dad, mom, or both.

Distinguish home and away. Most parents I have talked with about cohabitation take this kind of approach to their children: "While you are here at home we can insist on certain rules and procedures. But now that you are away from home at college or working in another city, we are not able to do that. You are on your own. We may not like or agree with your decision, but we must live with that. We also may express our displeasure and disagreement in the way we visit or do not visit your apartment or house. However, when you are here for vacation or a holiday, we will not permit you to sleep together in our house."

Form a united front. Both parents ideally should talk this matter through and arrive at a consensus about how they will react to their children's actual or potential cohabitation.

Years ago during a Sunday homily on cohabitation, I remember an obviously agitated father moving his leg back and forth. I also observed the mother gently patting his knee in an effort to ease her spouse's distress. Their daughter had recently moved in with her fiancé prior to the marriage.

It was several years later that I learned the reason behind his response to my words about living together. Their daughter's actions had deeply troubled him and he would not visit their apartment until after the marriage. His wife and her mother? Did she call upon her daughter at that apartment? I do not know. My guess is she did. Generally mothers will be mothers, even if they might disagree and disapprove of their daughter's actions.

Avoid playing God. For all the reasons outlined in the earlier chapters of this section, living together before marriage is, objectively, a moral wrong. Engaging in sexual intercourse prior to the nuptial vows increases the wrongness of that situation.

But subjective sin represents a different matter. Sin occurs when we fail to follow the divine imperative in our heart. Sin happens when we know something is wrong and freely choose that course of action. Sin means we have failed to follow our conscience.

The pervasive and powerful impact of our culture upon the couple certainly confuses the issue for them. In addition, the high incidence of premarital sex and cohabitation among peers further clouds their vision of what is right or wrong, wise or unwise in this matter.

The consciences of cohabiting couples are thus objectively in error; those in responsible positions like parents need to speak the truth to them, seeking to correct such erroneous judgments.

But some parents go beyond that and declare: "You are living in sin. You have seriously sinned. You must go to confession now. You may not go to communion until you have seen the priest and been forgiven."

Statements and comments like that cross the line. Parents are now playing God, mixing objectively wrong actions with personally subjective sin. Only the Creator can judge the sinfulness of an individual action.

Do not blame yourselves. Most parents I know torture themselves with guilt when faced with an unwed teenage pregnant daughter, an adolescent son on drugs, or offspring now married but who seldom attend church and have neglected the baptism of their infants. Many moms and dads with whom I am in contact suffer similar guilty pangs about their cohabiting children.

Generally speaking, these are instances of false, irrational, and unfounded guilt. They have been exemplary and conscientious parents. However, the weaknesses of human nature and the quicksand pull of contemporary culture are formidable opponents.

If parents have done their best by good example and wise guidance, then such dads and moms need to let go of this debilitating guilt. After all, they can give their children only roots and wings; they merely point the way, teach them to fly and release them to the world.

They surely may feel sad and wounded about the cohabitation. But it would be a mistake for them also to bear the burden of guilt.

Show constant and unconditional love. It should be clear that there are serious moral and practical negative dimensions to cohabitation. Yet, for those couples who will marry in the immediate or near future, this is a temporary concern. They will be righting the wrong at that time.

Moreover, even in today's worrisome pattern of cohabitation without any thought of marriage, a son remains a son and a daughter, a daughter.

God's love for us is constant, unconditional, and not dependent upon how good or bad we are, how well or poorly we keep the commandments. That divine steadfast, never ceasing love is most uniquely and effectively communicated through a similar love shown by parents to their children.

In summary, we recommend to parents: teach, warn, even contradict, but love them regardless of their currently perhaps bad choices.

A mother, concerned about her own daughter, sent me this story taken off the Internet. It makes, I think, a fitting conclusion to these words about parents and their cohabiting children.

THE ROOMMATE

John invited his mother over for dinner. During the meal, his mother couldn't help noticing how beautiful John's roommate Julie was. She had long been suspicious of a relationship between John and his roommate, and this only made her more curious.

Over the course of the evening, while watching the two interact, she started to wonder if there was more between John and the roommate than met the eye. Reading his mom's thoughts, John volunteered, "I know what you must be thinking, but I assure you, Julie and I are just roommates."

About a week later, Julie came to John and said, "Ever since your mother came to dinner, I can't find the beautiful silver gravy ladle. You don't suppose she took it, do you?"

John said, "Well, I doubt it, but I'll write her a letter just to be sure."

So he sat down and wrote, "Dear Mother, I'm not saying you did take a gravy ladle from my house and I'm not saying you did not take a gravy ladle, but the fact remains that one has been missing ever since you were here for dinner. Love, John."

Several days later, John received a letter from his mother which read, "Dear Son, I'm not saying that you do sleep with Julie, and I'm not saying that you do not sleep with Julie. But the fact remains that if she was sleeping in her own bed, she would have found the gravy ladle by now. Love, Mom."[1]

COUPLES AND THE CLERGY

When Rebecca, twenty eight, and Edward, thirty, met with the priest to arrange their wedding date, they were excited, but somewhat nervous. As he entered information about them in the reservation book, they gave an identical address and phone number for their residence. The priest said nothing and displayed no response. Instead, he spent the next hour first inviting them to talk about their lives and their courtship and then outlining many details about the needed church records and civil license, flowers and music, preparation programs and liturgical options, the usual offering and several future meetings.

Their excitement grew as the dreams of a wedding began to take actual shape and their nervousness started to ease significantly. With all that material covered, the priest, who had known Rebecca since childhood days, sat back and asked them: "Tell me about how you happened to move in together."

They explained: Edward's sister owned a home in the city and her tenant had just vacated the house. Rebecca still lived with her parents and found that difficult at twenty eight, but could not afford to rent an apartment alone. Both of them moving into the empty house therefore seemed to make sense and solve problems.

"How did your parents react?"

Rebecca replied that her mom was fairly comfortable with it, but her dad became very upset over the cohabiting. In fact, he would not tell anyone that his daughter was simply living with her boyfriend. Once they became engaged, his disapproval lessened, but he remained clearly unhappy with the situation.

This discussion surfaced the fact that their nervousness stemmed mainly from the cohabiting issue. They expected the priest to address the question and anxiously wondered what he would say or even do in response.

If cohabiting necessarily impacts the relationship of the couple to their parents, it obviously affects more the couple's connection with the clergy. That is, it will be a factor in their discussions unless they seek to conceal the living together arrangement—something that is difficult to achieve on a long-term basis and that is questionable to pursue in terms of basic honesty or integrity.

Most cohabiting couples, consequently, must face the question of meeting with the clergy and of wondering what to expect from them. As in the previous section, we think the following information may be helpful in that regard. The majority of clergy have in effect likewise read these words or studied this data.

As you glance through the extensive material below, once again imagine you are the clergy person reading or hearing these ideas. That process should, as with the parents, help you understand "where they are coming from."

This may reduce some of your own nervousness when you approach the clergy to arrange your wedding.

Cohabiting couples who come to the parish office and seek to make arrangements for a marriage, if they acknowledge their living together state, present the clergy with a difficult dilemma.

The priest, deacon, or pastoral minister wishes to be warm and welcoming, to rejoice with the couple over their great love for each other, and to begin the wedding preparation process on a positive note. At the same time, the clergy need to be true to Christ, faithful to the Church's teaching and clear about the negative moral and practical aspects of cohabitation.

Several decades ago, the clergy generally overlooked living together situations. After all, the instances were relatively rare and, moreover, the couples were now doing the right thing—correcting the situation by getting married.

But the geometrical growth of cohabitation over the past twenty to thirty years which we have outlined has led many religious leaders to re-examine their pastoral approach. Should they not confront the couple and correct them, even if they do resist the correction and resent the confrontation?

In 1984, an action by Father Thomas Kramer, rector of Holy Spirit Cathedral in Bismarck, North Dakota first publicly surfaced this growing uneasiness among clergy and developing shift in pastoral practice. His letter to couples living together was picked up by a syndicated religious news service and received widespread attention. Here is his letter in its entirety.

Dear Friends,

You have asked me to witness your marriage and I am pleased that you wish to be married in the church. Before I give you my answer about witnessing your marriage I want to share a few thoughts with you.

I am sure that you know that the church does not approve of your living together before marriage, and I hope you are not surprised that I also disapprove of it. By asking me to witness your marriage with the usual kind of wedding celebration, you are putting me in an awkward position. I feel that if I do witness the vows in a big celebration I am giving tacit approval to your present behavior. I would be treating you in the same way as I would treat a couple who has not been living together. I am uncomfortable with that because I want to encourage young people to live up to Catholic Christian standards before marriage.

Let me try to explain why I think that what you are doing is wrong. I don't want to talk just in terms of the commandments, though I believe what you are doing is contrary to them. I would rather talk about your relationship to the community—both the civil community and the church community. Both these communities disapprove of couples living together prior to marriage.

By your living arrangements, you are saying quite publicly that you don't care very much what these communities think. And yet, now you come to me, an official in the church community, and ask me to treat you in the same way I would treat a couple who had respected the community's customs and rules.

Putting it another way, you have been living as if married, in effect saying to the community, to your friends and your families, that you wish to be treated as if married—at least you want to live that way. But now, you come and say you want to be treated as unmarried and have a big celebration of the fact that you are now marrying. There is some kind of contradiction here, and it puts me in a difficult spot. If I say yes, I seem to be saying that what you are doing is okay. If I say no, I am refusing to help you get back into the community.

I think that living together and sexual relations prior to marriage are wrong. Sexual relations is a sign and symbol of a total gift of one person to another. That total gift is made in the marriage vows in which two people give themselves publicly and irrevocably to each other for life. To engage in sexual relations before making that formal, public, permanent gift and commitment in marriage is to falsify the sacred symbol that sexual intercourse is. It is to give yourself in this act that symbolizes total giving, but which in this case can be reversed because you haven't given yourself to each other in marriage. We don't like people who give gifts and then take them back. Even children see the error in that; but premarital sex can too easily become such a gift, which can be taken back.

God's laws regarding sexual behavior are not whimsical or arbitrary. They are guidelines to the deep significance of sexuality in our lives. They recognize the profound sacredness of our sexuality and are directly opposed to the cheap, selfish and shallow view of sexuality that is found in so much of our culture.

I think I can understand the social and economic pressures and your own feelings that have led you to live together. I would like to hear your reasons, but I am convinced that another solution could have been found—and even still can be—that will permit me to witness your marriage.

I would be happy to witness your marriage in a simple, quiet ceremony with two witnesses and perhaps your immediate families. That is what I would do if you had been married in a civil ceremony and now wished to have the marriage validated in the church.

By your living together you seem to be saying, "We want to be like married people." I would be very happy to treat you like married people, and witness your vows simply and quietly.

But I have serious difficulties with treating you like any other couple wishing to be married, who has not been living together.

Another possible solution might be for you to live separately from now until marriage. That would be a public statement to your family, your friend, and to me that you are trying to live your courtship in a Catholic way.

I hope you will think about these things. I also hope you will come to see me again and that we can work out some way that will allow me to witness your marriage.

I am happy that you love each other, and that you wish to marry. I hope that we can work out the difficulties that I have had with your present living arrangements.

I hope to hear from you soon.[2]

Around the same time that Father Kramer's letter appeared in newspapers across the country, Bishop George Speltz of the St. Cloud, Minnesota diocese issued a "Pastoral Letter on Cohabitation." After outlining the basic church teaching on living together which we detailed in the last chapter, he established the following policy for his diocese:

1. When marriage preparation begins, the priest is to determine whether or not the couple is living together.
2. If couples intending marriage are living together, they are to begin living separately immediately.
3. If they do not comply, the priest shall refuse to witness the marriage. If, however, the priest deems it advisable for compelling pastoral reasons that the marriage should take place:
    a) The celebration of the sacrament shall be in private in the presence of the witnesses and the immediate families.
    b) The parish facilities will be available to the wedding party and the immediate families only.
    c) The couple is bound to all the guidelines of the existing marriage policy of the diocese.[3]

While there was good support for the statements and policy of the St. Cloud bishop, few other dioceses adopted or developed similar documents or regulations.

The reasons for their hesitation to implement identical rules were many, such as: uneasiness about intruding upon the couple's natural right to marriage; concern over lack of honesty and true communication between clergy and couples; fear of the couple's and the family's permanent alienation from the church.

Instead, more and more dioceses envisioned the exchange between couple and clergy as a teachable and touchable moment. Recognizing that cohabitation is not an official impediment to marriage, these leaders encouraged a dialogue between the couple hoping to marry and the priest or deacon arranging the nuptial service. To facilitate that process, these leaders created a series of penetrating, but appropriate questions for the couple's self-examination and their subsequent discussion with the priest.

Most of these inquiries have been integrated into the series of questions for couples which conclude this section.[4]

In the 1997 sixth revised edition of my own book, *Together for Life*, used each year by perhaps a majority of couples being married before a Catholic priest, a new commentary "Living Together," contains several comments about cohabitation and also the seven questions which appeared in the American Bishops' "Catholic Handbook of Pastoral Help for Marriage Preparation."[5]

As we move into the new millennium some additional church guidelines and directives have surfaced to help the clergy respond to this current issue of cohabitation.

The American Bishops' Marriage and Family Committee in 1999 produced a very rich "Information Report" on the topic. It has been a significant source of data for chapters four and five of this book. However, it also contains several pages of practical, pastoral suggestions for the clergy and other parish leaders working with engaged couples or couples simply in love.[6]

In the same year, The Bishops of Pennsylvania, through its Pennsylvania Catholic Conference, produced an attractive, illustrated booklet, *Living Together*, "Questions and Answers Regarding Cohabitation and the Church's Moral Teaching." The answer to the first of ten questions defines cohabitation or living together as "the relationship of a man and woman who are sexually active and share a household, though they are not married." The other nine questions cover inquiries couples would frequently pose about cohabitation. The booklet concludes with eight questions for reflection and prayer.

The Pennsylvania bishops clearly presume that the clergy and pastoral leaders in their state will use this pamphlet in marriage preparation efforts.[7]

My own approach to cohabitation is this:

First of all, the matter needs to be addressed much earlier than when a couple arrives at the parish office to arrange their marriage. In some ways, it is by then already too late to make much of a difference.

Early teaching and preaching should, in the long term, help. A homily once or twice a year can deal with various aspects of cohabitation, including the role of parents. Confirmation sessions, high school religion classes, and marriage courses in college are a few obvious venues for positive, yet realistic teaching about living together. I would think that there is ample material in this section for many homilies, classes, and talks on cohabitation.

When uninvolved young persons have heard these words for a number of years from the pulpit or classroom, from a preacher or teacher, then when the suggestion or possibility of living together seems an attractive option, they may think twice about making that choice. Repeated preaching and teaching we trust will give them deeply entrenched facts, concepts and principles to make wise judgments and not yield to the immediately alluring decision to move in with someone they love.

Secondly, when the living together situation of the engaged couple surfaces at our initial interview—and there have been many over the past decade—I let it pass until after about an hour of that session (which lasts two hours). By then we know one another better; I trust that they feel loved and welcomed; the couple actually see the marriage being booked; they hear the details about music, license, preparation courses, documents, liturgy, and so on.

The dialogue would then follow something like this:

I take a deep breath, sit back and gently ask: "Tell me why you decided to move in together."

Normally the couple will respond quite openly about their motives and reasons.

"Were you expecting me to talk about your living together?"

They usually give an affirmative nod or even make a comment about their nervousness over the situation.

"Well, as you know, the church, for very good reasons, frowns on couples living together before marriage. If I didn't mention this now here is what might happen. Tomorrow, you will be talking to your close friends and with excitement describe this visit and the marriage plans. They will probably say: 'Did you tell him you were living together?' 'Yes.' 'Did he say anything?' 'No.'

I thus have given tacit public approval to your living together."

I would then reiterate my loving acceptance of them, assure them that the marriage will take place regardless, describe some of the reasons why the church opposes cohabitation and urge them to read and reflect on the section in *Together for Life* "Living Together."

I conclude the discussion by citing the suggestion of a midwest Cathedral rector for living together couples. "Since you don't think it is possible for you to separate before marrying, at some time prior to the wedding you might consider abstaining from sex. During Lent we usually give up something that we enjoy to help us become better persons in prepararation for Easter. Refraining now from sexual intercourse before your marriage would be something like that. In this way, the night of the wedding will not be the same as the night before the wedding."

Their usual response to that recommendation is, as one might anticipate, a rather blank stare, hardly enthusiastic. We then move on with the evening as they watch a marriage preparation video and complete FOCCUS, the communication skill-building questionnaire.

Pope John Paul II offers this advice to clergy and pastoral personnel who work with cohabiting couples. After recommending that they examine each situation case by case, the Holy Father encourages these leaders to make "tactful and respectful contact with the couples concerned and enlighten them patiently, correct them charitably, and show them the witness of Christian family life is such a way as to smooth the path for them to regularize their situation."[8]

GUIDELINES FOR COUPLES

There are three situations in which these particular guidelines for couples may have value: the couple in love who are contemplating cohabitation; the couple already living together who are pondering whether, in view of many factors, it might be better to separate; the couple who judge it is not really feasible for them to move apart, but who now consider refraining from sexual intercourse until their marriage.

Become informed. Making any major decision in our lives should be done with care, not casually, and based on solid facts, not only upon emotional desires. Couples who have read through this section already possess a substantial amount of that information which can help them make an informed choice.

Consult your parents. Parents know their children better than anyone else does. They can also detect trends or recognize signs that a daughter or son may fail to realize because of their already deep involvement. Moreover, the parents' support of or opposition to any decision about cohabitation will impact the couple's own relationship afterward. Thus, discussing this matter with parents is a wise move on many counts.

Consider the impact of living together on any children you may have. I mean by this that the couple consider the negative impact of cohabitation upon children. In the Rutgers National Marriage Project cited earlier, the authors propose four principles, based on their research, which seem best to prepare child-rearing couples for the long-term committed relationship of marriage.

They are: Consider not living together at all before marriage. Do not make a habit of cohabiting because there are unique dangers in multiple living-together experiences. Limit cohabitation to the shortest possible time. Do not cohabit if children are involved.

In connection with their fourth or last principle, the scholars argue that children need and should have parents who are committed to staying together for the long term. They also note that cohabiting parents break up at a much higher rate than married parents with possible devastating and often long-lasting negative effects upon the children. There is also a higher risk of sexual abuse and physical violence, including lethal violence, to children of parents living in cohabiting unions than to children living with married parents.[9]

Ask God for guidance. The decision to move in or to move out, to be sexually active or to practice premarital chastity, are very significant choices with substantive consequences on the rest of one's life. They presuppose sound insight and require a certain heroism to carry out.

God promises both. The Lord who is all-wise and all-powerful, who is beyond us and yet close to every person, who is incomprehensible but still most compassionate, who is especially near to the brokenhearted and the crushed in spirit, offers to every person divine wisdom and guidance, courage and strength. Furthermore, the Creator assures us that these gifts will be sufficient to meet our needs, just enough to make the proper decisions and to implement them. Moreover, Jesus promises great peace for those who do what is right.

The only requirement is that we must ask. The Bible repeatedly makes both this promise and this requisite. Ask, seek, and knock, Christ said, and you will receive, find, and have the door opened to you (Lk 11:9-10). "If you ask anything of me in my name, I will do it" (Jn 14:14). "My grace is sufficient for you, for power is made perfect in weakness" (2 Cor 12:9). "Peace I leave with you; my peace I give to you" (Jn 14:27).

Asking God frequently and regularly, with faith, opens the doors of a couple's heart to the divine wisdom and strength so abundantly available.

Some years ago a young military officer from Texas described the journey that he and his girlfriend followed prior to their marriage. Their scenario illustrates some of the guidelines for couples that are outlined here.

> I was involved in a relationship that was really pretty good in all respects. After six months, the growth of this relationship stopped. I really was not sure what I should do, but I knew that I liked this relationship and that it could possibly develop as a lasting one.
>
> My girlfriend and I decided not to "sleep" together any more. It really took a lot of discipline, but we figured it would pay off in the long run, no matter what became of the relationship. Time passed and the desire to be "together" was strong, but because we had committed ourselves to this special agreement we were successful. It felt like we were doing something together, as one, to strengthen our relationship. We found that our relationship had grown more in one month than over the first six months combined. We had discovered a new life within our relationship.
>
> A month had passed when I realized that I did indeed love my girlfriend. The love was strong and had grown stronger by the weeks. We developed a great deal of respect and found many new and wonderful things about each other. The relationship had come alive. Sex no longer seemed as desirous because we were having so much fun learning new things about each other and ourselves.
>
> The next great thing to happen to us was our new relationship, together, with God. This really put our relationship on an even stronger foothold. We could barely believe how great a relationship we had. We were so proud of ourselves and of each other. When our relationship did hit a low point, which I feel all

relationships will at some time, we recalled experiencing the beauty and gratification of a full relationship. The low point quickly passed and the relationship actually became stronger. With a strong faith in our relationship and God we realized that our life together could and can overcome anything.

From a small agreement and commitment between two adults came an incredibly wonderful relationship based upon mutual respect for each other and upon a faith that God will be with us at all times. My girlfriend will no longer be my girlfriend; she will be my wife in a few months.[10]

Having completed this section responding to the basic inquiry, "Should We Live Together First?" I now provide a series of questions for couples in love. The first three have been designed for those couples not living together, but who may be contemplating that step. The last seven are meant for couples intending to marry, but who are already living together.

QUESTIONS FOR REFLECTION

1. What reasons would you give to support a decision about moving in together? How do those resonate with the facts, reflections, and guidelines on cohabitation in Part Two of this book?
2. Have you discussed this with both sets of parents? If so, what did they say? How would they feel about your moving in together?
3. Is God part of this picture? In other words, are you regularly and frequently asking with faith for divine guidance and strength?

* * *

4. Why did you choose to live together (e.g., fear of permanent commitment, testing the relationship, concern about future divorce, convenience, need for companionship, financial reasons, escape from home)?
5. What have you learned from this experience of living together?
6. Can you identify the driving force or forces behind your decision to marry at this time?
7. Was there a previous reluctance or hesitation to marry? If so, why? Are you now at a new point of personal development? Have you completely resolved those previous issues?
8. What is it that prompts you to marry in the Catholic church at this time? Or, to place it in another context, why have you approached a Catholic priest or deacon now?
9. How do you envision marriage as a sacrament or sacred union for you?
10. Do you consider openness to life, growth in faith, and deepening of love as being an intimate part of your marriage?

PART THREE
WILL YOU MARRY ME?

CHAPTER 7

GOOD OLD DAD (OR MOM)

A s we begin this third part of the book, we shift gears a bit. In the first two sections we looked at the questions couples ask on the journey toward marriage: "Is this the person for me?" and "Should we live together first?" During that searching time you certainly have talked about married life in general, sharing your thoughts and feelings on what makes a marriage satisfying, good, and successful. Very likely you have also discussed your own possible married life in particular, even to the point of projecting future time frames, living arrangements and work situations.

But even though your marriage seems both desirable and almost certain, there still remains considerable hesitation and tentativeness until the actual proposal is made and accepted. This last part of the book is about that very question: "Will you marry me?" We will examine the how, where, and when of a marriage proposal and do so through the examples of more than a dozen couples who recently became engaged. We start the discussion with another story.

Our Saturday maintenance man, Jack Anson, has listened to many wedding homilies over the past several years. Prior to nuptial services, he arranges all the details around the altar. Following each particular celebration, he cleans up the sanctuary and church, often preparing for the second and third weddings which begin almost immediately.

During the weddings, however, he frequently sits in the custodian's office, turns on the loudspeaker there, and listens to what is happening in the church. That includes, of course, the homily and, in a majority of cases, the hopes and expectations which bride and groom have written for each other.

Jack was particularly struck by the words of Ken, a CPA who has worked for about a half dozen years as an auditor in one of America's large accounting companies. As the priest read Ken's hopes and expectations, Jack thought of his own proposal and of the early period in his own marriage with Gloria, his spouse now for nearly a half century. The groom's words were:

> It did not take long for Maureen to realize that it was difficult for me to display and express my emotions, my feelings, and my love to her. At times, she would get frustrated at my lack of affection and emotions and would take it very personally. I had to explain that it was not because of her that I did not show my feelings, but it was because of what I had seen over the years: friends that disregard their wedding vows and their families that were broken apart because of it; dating over the years which was filled with lies and deceptions; an occupation (auditing) where we are required to be what is called a professional skeptic, or basically taking caution in every single word that a client says to us; a society where all we hear on the news is the death, destruction, and the problems and issues that we have to face every day; all of this added together made me the hard-hearted person that I was. And then I met Maureen, the sweetest, most caring, loving, and sharing person I have ever met since mom. She brought

it all back to me, what it means to be a human, what it means to trust people, and what it means to see the best in all people.

My hopes and expectations are that she continues this throughout our lives together. For example . . .

When I come home from a difficult day at work, comfort me by letting me know that day is done and tomorrow is just hours away.

When it rains outside on my day off, remind me that it is good for our garden and that our flowers will grow.

When our children are being fresh, remind me that it is retribution for the years that we tortured our parents.

When I am asked to work on a weekend, remind me of my vacation days that I have left.

When I have to drive hours for work, remind me to check out the fall foliage on the way, the colors in the leaves, and the beauty in the landscape.

When I miss the children's ball game, remind me of the parent-teacher conference I can attend the next night.

When I begin to lose my balance in life, continue to be the foundation that holds me up.

Basically, keep being yourself every day for the rest of your life; the sweetest, most caring, loving, and sharing person I know. For this is why I will love you and will cherish you forever, and the reason why I am marrying you today.

His bride Maureen has worked for nearly a decade as a waitress in a franchise restaurant of a well-know national chain. She loves the job—the service dimension of it, the familiar exchange with regular customers, and the interesting encounters with new patrons.

Her words, also read by the priest as part of the homily, were fewer in number, but equal in intensity of love and admiration:

Kenneth,

> *Today is the start of our new life together as one. We will cherish this day for the rest of our lives. I cannot begin to tell you how long I've dreamed of meeting you at the altar and saying, "I do!" You are everything I've always wanted in a man and more. A best friend to me is someone who is understanding, caring, loving, and supportive, and you are all the above. You are truly a gift from God, and I thank him every day for bringing you into my life. I look forward to growing old with you and still having these strong feelings as I do for you today. I look forward to the wonderful experience of bringing children into this world with you by my side. You will make an excellent father and husband. I am so grateful to have you in my life. You truly make my life complete.*
>
> *I love you with all my heart, Kenneth.*
>
> *Love always,*
>
> *Maureen*

We live, obviously, in a new age with new customs and new traditions. However, my experience in the past decade indicates that many, actually the vast majority of engaged couples, are anxious to carefully observe older wedding customs and traditions.

For example, the groom is preoccupied with *not* seeing the bride prior to the service's start (even though they may have lived together for a year or two beforehand). The bride wants dad or mom or both to escort her down the aisle. The maid of honor judges that her serious duty is to care for the bride's long train. The best man knows that he must carry and produce the rings at the right time (without dropping them).

At the reception, the photographer and/or banquet director invariably guides the new husband and wife through countless long-standing customs—the toast, the first dance, the cake cutting.

A nuptial tradition I thought might no longer be operative was the custom of the groom asking permission from one or both of the bride's parents to marry their daughter. I was wrong.

Only a handful have neglected to contact good old dad (or mom) in advance and seek approval, blessing, or permission. Moreover, only in an isolated case or two did I detect any resentment about the practice, as if this was an outdated procedure, one which demeaned the bride's independence and displayed an unhealthy control of parent over daughter.

Kenneth did contact Maureen's parents prior to proposing in the kitchen. Here are stories of how three other grooms-to-be contacted either father, mother, or both and asked for their daughter's hand in marriage.

A MOTORBOAT, A TUXEDO, AND A POEM

Michael's job as busboy for a sorority at the University of Maryland was practically perfect: good food, decent wages, and best of all, an opportunity to mix with a group of attractive, young women. However, it turned out to be even more perfect than he had anticipated. Michael met Ines, one of the sorority members. They fell in love, he subsequently proposed to her, and now they have been married for over four years.

His plan for the proposal had a uniqueness to it, and to execute it he visited with Ines' mother a month in advance.

During that exchange he naturally sought her permission and blessing, but Michael also needed her cooperation. She had to keep his intentions a secret, he told her, and not tell Ines' father lest he betray the elaborate scheme due to his excitement.

Supposedly she withheld the news, although if the truth be known, I would wager Ines' mother, with the most stern of warnings, did let dad know. Not many spouses, in my experience, are able to keep such supposedly secretive information from each other.

Mike and Ines, with their families, annually spend some summer vacation time at a massive cottage on the bay side section of Ocean City, Maryland. As many as six families gather there for those occasions with upwards of fifty people present. It was on one of those days that Mike chose to make his proposal for marriage.

On the appointed date Mike told Ines that he was going to play golf with a group of his buddies. Instead, in the prearranged scenario, he rented a boat, donned a tuxedo, and with the help of those "golfing" friends made his way to the summer home by the bay. Mike's mother also playing a key role, suggested at the appropriate time that Ines might want to go down to the dock.

There, surrounded by fifty family members and friends, a totally stunned Ines saw her tuxedo-clad beloved standing in the boat with a piece of paper in hand.

Mike then read a poem describing their relationship that included these words:

> I remember the first time we met,
> over your dirty dinner plate,
> and later that semester when I was
> your busboy date.
> Ines, our relationship has just begun.
> My mom and dad would agree
> I have chosen the right one.

There is only one question I ask of thee—
Ines, I love you, will you marry me?

She nodded yes and wept. The assembled crowd applauded and shouted their approval. And an alerted participant captured it all on videotape. The framed poem hangs in their home and each year they review the wedding album, replay videos of their nuptual service as well as reception, and, thanks to the on-the-spot videographer, revisit the marriage proposal made from a boat on the bay in Ocean City, Maryland.

TWO GLASSES OF WINE

Morris, in his mid-thirties, is an engineer with a construction corporation; Rosemary, in her late twenties, is the human resources director for a health care company.

As the time to make a marriage proposal drew near, Morris called her father and invited him to lunch. Rosemary's dad, a factory worker on a night schedule, instead suggested that he stop at the house for a visit.

Somewhat anxious, Morris began talking about how wonderful the man's daughter was, how much he cared about her, and how he would like to spend the rest of his life with Rosemary. During this conversation, the father was reading the sports page of the daily paper and paying only half-attention to the earnest lover's words—until the last part of his semi-rehearsed speech.

"What did I just hear you say? Do you mean you want to marry Rosemary? Are you going to propose? I must call my wife and tell her the news!"

Now very excited, he put down the paper, picked up the phone, and called his wife Mary Ann at work. Morris tried to temper the father's enthusiasm and said he would like to keep this a secret until the actual proposal planned for a week later. That is a huge request for an Italian father and an extended Italian family.

A few days afterward, with seemingly everyone aware of Morris' plan except Rosemary, the two of them took a long drive. In the car Morris seemed pensive, anxious, and quiet. Several times Rosemary tried to start a conversation, but with no success. She had learned through other relationships and during her courtship with Morris that at times one or the other may simply not be in the mood to talk. After all, communication often does happen in silence and merely being present can forge a closer bond with each other.

At dinner, Rosemary sensed the same unusual nervousness on his part. Following the meal, Morris suggested that they have an after dinner drink. He had brought along a bottle of red wine and two glasses. He filled each with wine.

Little did she know that an artisan had earlier etched messages halfway down the side of each glass. Morris' contained the evening's date; Rosemary's read: "Will you marry me?" They did the usual toast and sipped a bit. He then said to Rosemary, "Did you notice the words on your glass?"

They have been married for two years now and are expecting their first child.

668 MILES

After Barry, twenty-seven, graduated from Slippery Rock College in Pennsylvania, he began teaching earth science at a public middle school north of Baltimore. A best friend asked him to be in his wedding. Barry agreed, not knowing that the rehearsal dinner, the church service, and the reception would change his life.

It was at those events that he met and instantly bonded with Michelle, twenty-two, a former Marist College student and a University of Maryland graduate with a master's degree in social work. She, too, was working in Maryland, but at Annapolis for the Department of Social Services in the foster care field.

A year or so later, during the summer, Barry had decided to propose, but wanted to visit with her parents beforehand. He was scheduled to join Michelle and her family for a week's vacation at the New Jersey shore. On the Friday three days prior to the vacation, Barry drove 334 miles one way to meet with her dad and mom for lunch.

He had enlisted the confidential assistance of Michelle's sister and husband to arrange this surprise noontime encounter with the father and mother. While Michelle's parents waited in the restaurant for her sister and her husband (by plan they never did show), they were stunned when Barry, in his Sunday-best clothes, walked in and nervously sat down.

The conversation went something like this:

"Barry, what are you doing here?"

"Well, I wanted to visit with you about a few things. As you know, Michelle and I are in a rather serious relationship. You need to know that she has changed my life; she has given me more joy than I thought possible; I can't tell you how important she is to me. I plan to propose soon."

"Barry, you didn't have to come up here just for this. Starting Monday we'll be together for two weeks at the shore and you could have talked with us then."

"No, this is a special event and I didn't want it to be merely another happening on an ordinary day at the ocean. I am not asking for your permission, but I do seek your blessing."

"You have that, of course, and we are thrilled. When will you propose?"

"This poses a little problem. I am not going to do it until after vacation. You'll have to keep this a secret."

Having delighted them with the announcement and yet burdened them with a confidence, he turned the car around and retraced the 334 miles. What makes this excursion even more impressive is the fact that Barry hates to drive.

Early that morning, Barry had told Michelle that he was going to a friend's farm and would help him harvest his crop of hay. To cover this misleading comment, before reaching her home, Barry stopped at his own place, changed into grubby clothes, rolled around in the dirt outside the apartment, and made his way to Michelle's place.

He proposed to Michelle several weeks later. And her parents kept the secret.

CHAPTER 8
A SPECIAL PLACE

As a high school student Janet became very skilled in karate and gained national recognition. To develop those abilities further and to prepare for perhaps a career as an instructor in karate, she entered a school in Buffalo.

Soon she met and fell in love with Jay, a young man from South Korea, also a karate student and instructor. For their subsequent marriage, Janet expressed in her own handwriting these hopes and expectations to be read as part of the wedding homily:

> *Dear Jay,*
>
> *I thank God for bringing you into my life every day! I am very much looking forward to being your wife and for you to be my husband. With you I have found my best friend for life! I hope and pray that we will be this happy or even happier for the rest of our lives. I am excited about starting our lives together. Of course, there are many things that I hope and pray for every day. Like my mom, I pray each night that God brings good people into my life and into the lives of those I love, and look . . . I have found you!*

I hope that one day we will be blessed with children and that we can raise them like you and I were raised by our families. I know that you and I will be wonderful parents; we have so much love to share. I hope that all of our dreams for a school become a reality for us. I expect things to be difficult and tight, but I also expect us to get through the tough times even stronger than when we started!

I hope that even in this crazy world we are living in our love can grow deeper and stronger year by year, month by month, day by day, minute by minute; and it will as long as we both continue to realize that this is not only a marriage of two but a marriage of three. You, myself, and our God. With God on our side nothing will fail us, and this I know from my twenty years with him so far. Thank you, Jay, for loving me and for being my rock. I am always and forever your partner for anything and everything that you may ever need. Thank you!

From the moment I saw you,
I wanted to meet you.
From the moment I met you,
I wanted to know you.
From the moment I knew you,
I was in love with you.
From the moment I loved you,
I wanted to share my life with you.
And from that moment to this moment,
And for all the moments to come,
I will love you with all my heart,
No matter what, no matter when!

Love always,
Janet

A contingent of about forty Korean guests heard these words and, with the others in attendance, applauded her very personal message.

Jay struggles a bit with English and used the computer to compose his own thoughts about their future. His ideas combined the real and the ideal, a recognition of the unique challenges they face, yet an expectation that their strong love would carry them through everything.

Dear Janet,

I am very happy to be here today to become your husband. I come here to make a promise to you, and to our family and friends that our life together will be forever, no matter what, no matter when. I thank you and your family for accepting me and always treating me as a member of your family.

I look forward to our life together expecting so many wonderful times together and working through the tough times. Such as you, an American girl, and me, a Korean boy with different cultures and expectations, but always working together to be positive.

I want to be the best husband and friend that I can be to you and someday to be a great father. I look at you and I see so many wonderful things. I see a friend who I can laugh with, someone that is always willing to care for me, and most of all I see a beautiful woman, not only on the outside, but in the inside as well. You have a heart that is filled with so much love and beauty.

I want our life together to be you and me as a team, always together. I look forward to spending the rest of my life with you, knowing that you and I as husband and wife will be one of a kind. I love you more that anything in the world. No matter what! No matter when!

Love always,
Jay

After the wedding, they traveled to South Korea for a month-long honeymoon in his native land.

In my experiences with the engaged, I find that almost every groom has given very careful consideration to the marriage proposal. The time, the process, the place—each of these had particular significance and unique meaning.

Just as Korea and Korean customs will always be a central factor in the married life of Janet and Jay, so certain locations possessed a specialized importance for the following three couples.

NEW YORK, NEW YORK

Jack went north to Syracuse University for his undergraduate studies and became a devoted "Orange" football fan. Jacqueline, on the other hand, following the tradition of father and grandfather, headed south to Georgetown for her college education.

After graduation they both found jobs in the corporate and financial world of New York City. Several mutual friends arranged for them to meet at a bar. They connected well, began dating, and three years later were thinking seriously of marriage. Jack in the meantime began an M.B.A. at Columbia.

Both were out of town for different weddings and business matters during the week of Jack's planned proposal. Upon their mutual return, he arranged for a deluxe dinner cruise around their beloved Manhattan on a Friday evening.

The nighttime views were spectacular; the gourmet dinner, superb; the wine, special. However, Jack had also organized an event equally spectacular, superb, and special.

As they prepared to dock, Jack asked Jacqueline to note a crowd of people on the shore holding a large banner with a message on it. The words were: "Jacqueline, will you marry me?" Typical of New York, the small prearranged group of friends had grown considerably, augmented by curious onlookers who enthusiastically joined the event when they learned about the proposal. Jack had also alerted the boat crew about his project.

He then knelt down by the table (astutely located next to a window) and proposed. When she said "yes," the ship gave a few blasts on its horn, waiters brought out champagne, the other diners applauded, and those on shore, realizing Jacqueline had accepted his proposal, shouted their approval.

Later, at the wedding, Jack shared some of his hopes for the future:

> *The evening that we first met, we talked for hours. Never had I felt so comfortable, so open, so able to easily share my feelings with anyone. Since then, our relationship has grown and blossomed. You are my greatest friend. Life has its ups and downs, and I know that things won't always be easy, but I look forward to having you there as a friend and a partner to have a shoulder to lean on when I need it, and to offer a shoulder when you need it.*

Jacqueline expressed her dreams in this way:

> *For over four years you have been the greatest presence in my life. I can never remember a time when I have laughed more or felt as happy about my future and myself. You have been a grounding force that has made me realize the things that are most important in life: good health, love, and family. Despite how I sometimes nag you or seem frustrated at the stupid things you do, you exceed all the expectations I have ever had for a boyfriend, fiancé, and now husband.*
>
> *At this time, it is difficult for me to clearly understand what my hopes and expectations are for our*

future together. I feel that we are at a crossroad, both personally and professionally. You will soon be finishing your graduate work and the resulting job change could take us anywhere, or maybe keep us in New York for many years. Furthermore, my work situation is changing every day and remains very uncertain. I cannot anticipate where I will be professionally in six months because of this merger, but one of the few things that has made me feel comfortable is your promise to be flexible to whatever changes are made to my career. I don't know many men who would be so accommodating, which is just another reminder why I love you so much.

Personally, my only expectation for our future is that we have a long life together, blessed with many friends, children, and grandchildren. I have learned that life can change at any moment and mock the plans that you have made. I know that whatever happens, I will be happy if I still have you by my side to love, and to love me in return.

THE SAME PARK BENCH

At age thirty-two, Mario had reluctantly resigned himself to a life without marriage. "I never dreamed," he said, "that I would meet and marry someone as wonderful as Angelina."

Both are optometrists and first connected while they worked at the same Veterans Administration health care facility. Both come from deeply traditional Italian families (at their wedding they would include prayers and readings proclaimed in Italian and Latin as well as English).

It was fitting, therefore, that they selected for their initial date an upscale Italian restaurant located on the outskirts of a lakeside village. This establishment has since gained recognition as the place where President Bill Clinton with his wife, daughter, and friends dined while vacationing on that beautiful lake.

After their meal, Angelina and Mario drove back to the village itself, left their car, and walked to the local park located by the water's edge. They sat on one of the benches for a long time talking, gazing silently at the stars, and inwardly rejoicing over this unexpected discovery of each other.

A year later, near the anniversary of their first date, Mario took his sweetheart to another restaurant near the lake—this one, however, on a summit with an exceptional view of the sparkling water below and the spectacular surrounding hillsides. He then drove to the village and suggested they sit for a while on that same park bench, the site of their original post-dinner exchange.

Some time later, nervous but excited, he knelt down and proposed. People around them in the park sensed what was happening and erupted into applause when the now engaged couple rose to their feet and embraced.

FAR ABOVE CAYUGA'S WATERS

Tony and Susan went to public high schools in the same city and actually began going together during those teen years.

After graduation, Tony, a very proficient swimmer, went off to a New England college on an athletic scholarship. He studied criminal justice with the intention of making law enforcement his career.

Susan entered the Industrial and Labor Relations School at Cornell because tuition in that division was ten thousand dollars less than the standard tuition at this Ivy League university. She planned to enter Harvard Law School after finishing her studies at Cornell.

Their courtship continued throughout those collegiate years. Tony intended to propose marriage when Susan graduated from Cornell. He wanted to do so in a semi-public fashion, not on a roadside billboard or during a baseball game, but in a way she would always remember.

He made several secret trips to Ithaca, New York, where the Cornell campus rests, according to its alma mater, "far above Cayuga's waters." After much negotiating with authorities, Tony finally persuaded an administrator to approve of his plan.

On graduation day, around two hundred and fifty students, with families and friends, assembled in the large auditorium to hear their names proclaimed and to receive their diplomas.

When the Industrial Relations director called Susan's name, Tony quickly made his way to the platform, knelt down, proposed, and gave her the engagement ring. The students, aware of Tony's plan, enthusiastically applauded his request and her acceptance.

Three years later, city police officer Tony waited at the altar for Harvard Law School graduate Susan to walk down the aisle. The question this time was posed by the officiating priest to the couple, not by Tony to his beloved.

"Have you come here freely and without reservation to give yourselves to each other in marriage?"

"Will you love and honor each other as husband and wife for the rest of your lives?"

"Will you accept children lovingly from God and bring them up according to the law of Christ and his church?"

CHAPTER 9

ON BENDED KNEE

Apharmaceutical saleswoman in her mid-thirties, Magdalene always wanted to marry but had grown discouraged through some unsatisfactory experiences with past relationships. In her frustration, she decided to put this matter in the hands of God and the Blessed Mother.

The very day she surrendered her concerns while at Mass, Magdalene stood for the greeting of peace, turned around, and there behind her was Gerald, a forty-year-old, unmarried physician she had met previously through business contacts.

They began to date and, although both were a bit wary because of their ages, individual personalities, and past experiences, they found an ease and closeness growing with each encounter.

Magdalene describes the first part of that journey:

> For many years I prayed that I would meet my soul mate. I watched couples interact, I researched how they met, and I asked questions about their feelings and hopes. As time went on, I had a pretty clear idea of the qualities I was looking for in my special someone.
>
> In February of 1996, I attended a goal-setting seminar. I was asked to write down what needed to happen

in my life in the next three years to be both profession-
ally and personally happy. Achieving my professional
goals took planning and perseverance; I found it easier
to do than achieving my personal goal of marrying a
kind, thoughtful, driven, faithful, Catholic man (that's
the short list). I knew in my heart God had a specific
plan for me, and that I had a tremendous amount of
love to give to the right man.

One Sunday in church, I had an animated discus-
sion with God about the fact that I was tired of the dat-
ing scene. I put the entire "project" in God's hands,
along with my trust. Five months short of my three-
year goal we met.

On our first date I was charmed at your intensity
and gentlemanly ways. I noted the loving way you
talked about your grandmother and that you were close
to your family like I am.

The initial date was a good start, but, having been
wounded and frustrated in previous relationships,
Magdalene turned to God and the Blessed Mother again
for guidance. Is this the right man? Am I making another
mistake? Should I proceed?

These thoughts were running through her mind as she
prayed the rosary on a morning trip over an interstate
highway en route to several potential customers.
Preoccupied with her prayerful pondering and focused on
the road ahead, Magdalene, at first, did not notice a phenomenon in the sky. Finally, looking up, she saw a magnif-
icent rainbow.

Rainbows for her, and for many persons, symbolize
God's presence in our lives. That connection has a good
biblical basis (in Genesis 9, God placed a rainbow in the
clouds as a sign to Noah of his covenant). The top of the
rainbow reaches into heaven and the two end points

plunge into earth, the divine merging, as it were, with our humanity, a loving God walking by our side.

The rainbow encouraged Magdalene that, yes, she was moving in a wise and right direction. She recounts how their courtship developed:

> *I knew you were a unique individual, so I proceeded. Your family and friends were so lovely. I saw this very accomplished and caring physician who needed to evolve and finally feel love. The more you received God's love and guidance, the more you opened up to me and to new experiences. I love you for that.*
>
> *Today, when I think about you I am excited to know I am marrying my soul mate: the one whom I admire, trust, pray with; make good decisions with, want to share a family with; the one who strives as I do to understand before being understood; the one I feel like a kid with when it's just us; the one I want to discover the world with for the rest of my life. And finally, YOU are the one person I want to set new three-year goals with to achieve personal happiness together.*
>
> *Much love,*
> *Magdalene*

Who was this physician, this intense gentleman who needed to evolve and finally feel love?

Gerald, at their wedding, had the priest read this remarkably frank self-disclosure about who he had been and what Magdalene has done for him.

> *Once upon a time there was a middle-aged man, lost in his thoughts and imbued with an understanding that somehow feeling and life were very dangerous. He was a rather eccentric duck. He could comfortably spend a lot of time by himself; he appreciated good*

wine and cigars, loved interesting conversation, had an extensive collection of documentary videos, and was neurotically obsessive about how he ordered the space around him. He was blessed with a great family, a fine office staff, and many wonderful friends. In his little universe he felt very safe and contented, but he was alone. He was remiss to venture out and found leaving his little world to be very frightening. He invented all kinds of excuses not do so, but this only served to intensify his own isolation.

One day there came into his life a tall, young sales-woman, who appeared very focused on her work. As he continued to get to know her he realized she had a keen practical mind offering quiet wisdom and insight. Over time her voice took on a soft melodious quality and gradually did the fog lift and he realized that what stood before his eyes was a very beautiful woman and, what's more, the strength, charm, and graciousness that marks refined womanhood. He grew to love her and she changed his world forever.

Magdalene, I am sure you recognize that this is our story and I think few, other than yourself, could have had the charity, patience, and insight to have made it happen. You had love strong enough to rescue me from myself. With an almost uncanny perception, could you decipher the workings of my mind and heart. But more than all this, you showed me how the simplest things in life could somehow be so lovely. Grow old with me and with God's help, may the best be yet to come.

The relationship of Gerald and Magdalene began on bended knees in a church at Mass. Most wedding propos-als do not take place in churches, but the groom-to-be usu-ally does get down on one bended knee when he asks his beloved to marry him. Gerald did just that, in his home, about a year after that first encounter in church.

CHRISTMAS EVE

The sour end of a serious relationship had left Stacey with strange feelings of disillusionment about men and with absolutely no desire to go out on a date. She was less than enthusiastic when her long-time girlfriend said: "I want you to meet this guy named Joe. I think the two of you would hit it off together very well. Will you join us for dinner or a drink?"

She reluctantly agreed to do so.

The rest, as they say, is history. Two years later they became engaged and two months later they sat down with the priest to arrange the wedding date and begin the marriage preparation process. For Joe, in his early thirties and middle manager for a finance company, this was the surprise realization of a dream from the distant past. He had a crush on Stacey ten years earlier although she did not recognize that then. College, graduate school, and work separated them for many years until the fateful dinner and drink.

They immediately bonded that night with the matchmaker girlfriend disappearing and the two of them talking for several hours. Stacey, in her mid-twenties and a nurse practitioner working at a hospital pulmonary unit, was both surprised and pleased when Joe asked: "Would you come to my house Thursday night? I will cook dinner for the two of us."

After the fine meal (both are Italians for whom food and family rate high on a priority list), Stacey and Joe sat on the back porch and talked until 4:00 a.m., covering every topic imaginable.

Much later, after an extended courtship, Joe knew that Stacey would like the engagement to be a major occasion. However, he preferred a private proposal to a public event.

Joe pondered at length how to mix the two apparently conflicting desires and finally decided to give her the diamond on Christmas Eve in his home.

They opted to open their personal presents during Christmas Eve day before making the mandatory visit to both families. With the exchanges completed ("He gave me some wonderful things"), Stacey stepped into the bathroom to put on makeup prior to leaving for both the family homes. Joe walked in, stood behind her as she was looking into the mirror, put his arms around Stacey, and held the open box with the diamond in it.

He could see the shock, smile, and tears in the mirror. She likewise through the mirror noted some glistening in his eyes. Joe then knelt down and formally proposed.

Stacey's father is a lawyer and Joe, on four afternoons in a row before Christmas, had stopped at his office to ask for her dad's permission. Unfortunately, on each occasion he was out and they never connected. Joe did not want to speak with him about this matter merely over the phone. Later, when the now engaged pair reached the families and announced the news, Joe explained to Stacey's father what had happened and expressed his regret about not making personal contact. Joe added, "When the time comes in the future for our own daughter to marry, I would like the man to come and tell me about his intentions."

A CLASSROOM PROPOSAL

Rachel and Sean appeared earlier in this book, although not identified by name. They were part of that group who gathered with me for a Sunday night dinner to discuss the forthcoming Christmas homily.

These couples agreed that time or, rather, lack of time seemed the greatest challenge facing people in our world today. Sean and Rachel, then engaged, commented on the stress of premarital arrangements and how their brief moments together were no longer just fun but always seemed filled with difficult discussions about wedding matters.

Rachel, with undergraduate and graduate degrees in special education, teaches in a public school where most of her students are troubled teenagers, many of whom have been incarcerated for significant offenses. Sean, an assistant district attorney, jokingly remarks that he convicts them and, after their release from prison, they end up in her classroom.

During the Christmas season, Sean was in a jewelry store looking for a diamond engagement ring. Unfortunately, Rachel stopped into the same place on that day with several friends for another reason and discovered Sean there. Totally surprised, she knew a proposal would be imminent, but had no idea when this would happen.

On the eve of Valentine's Day, Sean visited Rachel's classroom. He often dropped in to see her and had developed an excellent rapport with her "special" students.

This dialogue ensued:

"What do you think I should give my girlfriend for Valentine's Day?"

"Diamonds!"

"Should I marry her?"

"Yes!"

"Do I give her a ring?"

"Definitely!"

"When?"

"Today, right now!"

"Where?"

"Here!"

Sean obeyed their urgent suggestions, knelt down on one knee, and proposed.

For the rest of the school day, I doubt if the joyfully excited teacher taught or the charged-up students learned very much.

Rachel and Sean are married now and have purchased a modest home. But they still wrestle with the same thorny issue that weighed upon those couples at the dinner months earlier. "How can we have one parent stay at home with the children and still make ends meet? Do I give up the district attorney post I love and enter the private sector? The money there will be greater, but the probably more intense time demands will cut into my presence with the family."

It remains to be seen how they will resolve that matter.

STARTING OVER

Kathleen grew up in a troubled home: her father departed when she was nine and her parents divorced when she reached eighteen. As is often the case, the parents' breakup caused Kathleen to feel rejected, anxious about divorce, and quite down on herself.

Eventually she gave up on her Catholicism, lost her faith, and finally married in a local community church. She had a daughter from this union, but soon a marital communication breakdown led to her own divorce.

A few years later, while working at a telephone company, she met Martin, a repairman for the same corporation. They began dating, fell in love, and started going to Mass together each Sunday.

Kathleen next completed the church annulment process that opened the door for her marriage to Martin. Both of them saw an advertisement from the area retreat house about an evening for couples in love which included Mass, dinner, and movie. They enjoyed the event and judged that it was $40 well spent. Martin gave her a cross and some earrings that night. However, they were uncertain whether the retreat house Mass fulfilled their Sunday obligation and decided to go to church the next day.

They took their usual front pew seat, and as they prayed before Mass Martin said that he had a gift for

Kathleen after the service. When the eucharist was over, she began to gather her belongings. Martin reminded her of his gift, asked her to kneel down with him, and there, in the church, proposed.

Months later, in a simple celebration with her daughter Kerry as the flower girl, they married. The are now regular Sunday Mass participants, take their turn as eucharistic ministers, and also serve every five weeks on a collection counting team. Kerry has made her first penance as well as first communion and is there for the eucharist and religious instruction each weekend.

Is this the person for me? Kathleen answered "yes" to that question a decade or so ago. However, her troubled background and deep insecurities no doubt affected the clarity of her vision and the accuracy of her judgment at that time. Now wounded, but wiser, her vision of a future with Martin and her judgment about their relationship is certainly clearer and better grounded.

She, of course, again responded "yes" to the question, "Is Martin the person for me?" But Kathleen did so with a much steadier confidence and stronger hope that they will be in love and together all the days of their lives, until death do they part.

QUESTIONS FOR REFLECTION

1. Have you, would you, will you connect with your intended's dad, mom, or both before the marriage proposal?

2. Do you see yourself at that time announcing an event, seeking permission, or requesting their blessing?

3. When a parent or parents escort the daughter down the aisle at a wedding, is that an unhealthy and outdated symbol of handing over ownership of a person or a sign of unselfish parental letting go and the loving presentation of a grown child to another?

4. Did the facts and reflections in this book concerning cohabitation affect your thinking about that matter?

5. What is the best approach for parents to take toward a daughter or son who is cohabiting before marriage?

6. Is abstaining from sexual intercourse for a period of time immediately prior to the wedding a wise and feasible step for cohabiting couples?

7. Can you recall the painful distance arising from a serious conflict and the renewed closeness emerging from a mutual reconciliation?

8. Does the daily ten-minute listening with love suggestion seem desirable and possible?

9. What does love in marriage mean to you?

ACKNOWLEDGMENTS

The written hopes and personal lives of the many engaged or married couples who appear in these pages form the heart of this book. I am deeply grateful for my positive encounters with them over the past decade and for their willingness to share themselves so openly with others in this way.

Mrs. Rosalie Brennan, with her questions in Part One, provides wise inquiries for wondering couples, and they come from a school counselor, married woman, and mother of two grown daughters. I thank her and her family for that dinner which early on gave a direction to my writing and led to those incisive questions.

Peter and Rosemary Carr, long-time friends, who sent me the Internet story of "The Roommate" for Part Two made it possible to bring that particular section to a poignant yet humorous conclusion. I appreciate very much their contribution.

Librarians Wendy Bousfield and Daniel Smith after an intensive search located the sole copy of *The Love Machine* to be found in the public libraries of Onondaga County. Their ready willingness to help and their remarkable ability to uncover relatively obscure items both encouraged and impressed me. My warm gratitude goes to both of them.

Caring and competent friends who read the first draft of a manuscript and respond with comments make a book better. In this category I list, with special appreciation, Father Donald Krebs, Ms. Patricia Livingston, Father John Roark, and Mrs. Ann Tyndall.

Our Auxiliary Bishop Thomas J. Costello not only checked the text for its orthodoxy, but with his gifted editorial eye suggested forty-two changes which significantly improved the book. He has been a close personal friend and colleague, supporter and guide for over fifty years.

Mr. Frank Cunningham and Mr. Robert Hamma, publisher and editorial director respectively at Ave Maria Press, spent three hours with me on a beautiful summer day in July at Notre Dame discussing the audience and thrust of this book. Their encouragement and direction were most helpful as I began Parts Two and Three.

Later, Bob's very thorough and superb editing together with Frank's sage advice meant the final product was far superior to the original draft. I want to thank them for their real interest and professional assistance at the beginning, in the middle and at the end of the writing process.

Finally, Art and Patricia Gale once again combined their talents and energies as husband and wife team to transfer my handwritten pages to computerized hard copy and disk. My gratitude goes to them not only for this project, but also for their support and collaboration over the past twenty years.

I hope and pray that many individuals and couples will find help here in dealing with those three questions about love, living together, and marriage.

Father Joseph M. Champlin
Cathedral of the Immaculate Conception
Syracuse, New York
All Saints' Day, 2000

NOTES

1. FRIENDSHIP

1. *Webster's Third New International Dictionary* (Springfield, MA: G. and C. Merriam Company, 1976), p. 911.

2. *The Art of Loving* by Erich Fromm (New York: Bantam Books, 1954), pp. 8, 18-19.

3. *The Greatest Generation* by Tom Brokaw (New York: London House, 1998), Jacket.

4. *Ibid*, pp. 18-24.

5. *The Art of Loving*, p. 18.

6. *Sabbatical Journey* by Henri J. M. Nouwen (New York: The Crossroad Publishing Company, 1998), p. 7.

2. COMMUNICATION

1. *The Notebook* by Nicholas Sparks (New York: Warner Books, Inc., 1996), pp. 166-167, 179, 182, 184.

2. *From the Heart* by Joseph M. Champlin (Notre Dame, IN: Ave Maria Press, 1998), pp. 13-15.

3. FORGIVENESS

1. *The Holy Longing* by Ronald Rolheiser (New York: Doubleday, 1999), pp. 3-4.

2. *Necessary Losses* by Judith Viorst (New York: Fawcett Gold Medal, 1986), pp. 2-5.

3. For Catholic teaching on original sin, see *Catechism of the Catholic Church*, Second Edition (Citta del Vaticano: Libreria Editrice Vaticana, 1997; and Washington, D.C.: United States Catholic Conference, 1997), articles 396-412.

4. My deep gratitude to John Lawyer of Hennebury Associates, 2844 Henneberry Road, Pompey, New York 13138 for the basic concepts behind this material.

5. *Bound to Forgive* by Lawrence Martin Jenco, O.S.M. (Notre Dame, IN: Ave Maria Press, 1995), pp. 13-14, 19-21, 113.

6. *The Gift of Peace* by Joseph Cardinal Bernardin (Chicago: Loyola Press, 1997), pp. 25-26, 34-41.

7. *Saints of the Roman Calendar* by Enzo Lodi, translated by Jordan Aumann, O.P. (New York: Alba House, 1992), pp. 177-178. Also, *Saint of the Day* by Leonard Foley, O.F.M., Editor (Cincinnati, Ohio: St. Anthony Messenger Press, 1990), pp. 158-159.

8. *A Path to Peace* by Joseph M. Champlin (Los Angeles: Franciscan Communications, 1983).

9. "Vows That Last" by Jeanne Albanese, *Syracuse Herald-American*, June 4, 2000, Section AA.

10. *Sabbatical Journey*, p. 178.

4. FACTS

1. *Faithful to Each Other Forever:* "A Catholic Handbook of Pastoral Help for Marriage Preparation," by Bishops' Committee for Pastoral Research and Practices of the National Conference of Catholic Bishops (Washington, D.C.: United States Catholic Conference, 1988). A section, "The Question of Cohabitation," pp. 71-77, summarizes well the scientific research and pastoral approach about this issue during the late 1980s.

2. "Marriage Preparation and Cohabiting Couples: Information Report," by the National Conference of Catholic Bishops' Committee on Marriage and Family (Washington, D.C.: U.S. Catholic Conference, 1999). Published in *Origins*, September 16, 1999 Vol. 29: No. 14, pp. 213-224. This remarkable document builds upon the treatment twelve years earlier in *Faithful to Each Other Forever* noted above. The impressive report provides updated statistical information and an overview of common pastoral approaches to cohabitation. This document and its predecessor *Faithful to Each Other Forever* are the sources for this section about the 1990s.

3. "Changing the Shape of the American Family" by Karen Peterson in *USA Today*, April 18, 2000, D 1-2.

4. "Living Together As Trial Run for Marriage Fails on Many Levels," by Laura Schlessinger in *Syracuse Post-Standard*, April 2, 2000, D-4.

5. *Parenthood by Proxy* by Dr. Laura Schlessinger (New York: Cliff Street Books, 2000).

6. *Should We Live Together?* by David Popenoe and Barbara Dafoe Whitehead (New Brunswick, NJ: The National Marriage Project, Rutgers, The State University of New Jersey, 25 Bishop Place, New Brunswick, NJ 08901). For more information on this study or copies of the publication, write to the New Brunswick address.

7. "Unmarried Couples Shouldn't Live Together," by Juli Loesch, in *U.S. Catholic*, July, 1985, pp. 16-17. Quoted in *Faithful to Each Other Forever*, pp. 73-74.

5. REFLECTIONS

1. "Marriage Preparation and Cohabiting Couples," pp. 218-219. This is the source for the first four points in this section on "Sociological Studies."

2. *Faithful to Each Other Forever*, p. 73.

3. Jimmy Breslin in *Once a Catholic* by Peter Occhiogrosso (Boston: Houghton Mifflin Company, 1987), p. 176.

4. *The Love Machine* by Jacqueline Susann (New York: Simon and Schuster, 1969), pp. 43-51.

5. "Genital Relationships: A Question of Integrity" by Martin Helldorfer appearing in *Sexuality* (Lockport, IL: Christian Brothers' Conference, 1977), p. 60.

6. *Catechism of the Catholic Church*, Second Edition, article 1605, p. 401.

7. *Ibid*, article 2367, p. 569.

8. "Latest Youth Trend Encouraging: Sex Can Wait" by Tom Kean and Isabel Sawhill in *The Washington Post*, appearing in the *Syracuse Herald-American*, Sunday, September 10, 2000, Section D, pp. 1, 5.

9. *Catechism of the Catholic Church*, article 2350, p. 564.

10. *Time*, August 28, 2000, Cover and pp. 46-55.

11. *Catechism of the Catholic Church*, article 2390, p. 575.

12. *Ibid.*, articles 1641-1642, pp. 409-410.

6. GUIDELINES

1. With the rapidly accelerating use of the Internet by Americans, attribution of material taken from that source is difficult, if not impossible. Such is the case with this amusing, but pointed story about a clever, concerned mother.

2. *Faithful to Each Other Forever*, pp. 74-75.

3. *Ibid.*, pp. 75-76.

4. *Ibid.*, p. 76.

5. *Together for Life* by Joseph Champlin (Notre Dame, Indiana: Ave Maria Press, 1970, 1997), P. 61.

6. "Marriage Preparation and Cohabiting Couples," pp. 219-222.

7. "Living Together" by the Bishops of Pennsylvania (Harrisburg, Pennsylvania Catholic Conference). Available from the Conference at 223 North Street, Box 2835, Harrisburg, PA 17105.

8. *Faithful to Each Other Forever*, p. 77.

9. *Should We Live Together?* By David Popenoe and Barbara Dafoe Whitehead.

10. *Faithful to Each Other Forever*, p. 77.

Fr. Joseph M. Champlin is the rector of the Cathedral of the Immaculate Conception in Syracuse, New York. He is the author of more than forty books, including two popular resources or marriage preparation: *Together for Life* and *From the Heart: Personalizing Your Wedding Homily With Your Own Hopes and Expectations.*